THE BEGINNER'S GUIDE TO THE

Akashic Records

THE BEGINNER'S GUIDE TO THE

Akashic Records

Understanding Your Soul's
History and How to Read It

Whitney Jefferson Evans

Adams Media
New York   London   Toronto   Sydney   New Delhi

Adams Media
An Imprint of Simon & Schuster, Inc.
100 Technology Center Drive
Stoughton, MA 02072

First Adams Media hardcover edition
January 2021

ADAMS MEDIA and colophon are
trademarks of Simon & Schuster.

For information about special discounts for
bulk purchases, please contact Simon &
Schuster Special Sales at 1-866-506-1949
or business@simonandschuster.com.

The Simon & Schuster Speakers Bureau can
bring authors to your live event. For more
information or to book an event contact the
Simon & Schuster Speakers Bureau at 1-866-
248-3049 or visit our website at
www.simonspeakers.com.

Interior design by Michelle Kelly
Interior images by Frank Rivera

Manufactured in the United States of
America

2 2022

Library of Congress Cataloging-in-
Publication Data
Names: Jefferson Evans, Whitney, author.
Title: The beginner's guide to the Akashic
records / Whitney Jefferson Evans.
Description: First edition. | Avon,
Massachusetts: Adams Media, 2021.
Identifiers: LCCN 2020035002 |
ISBN 9781507214336 (hc) | ISBN
9781507214343 (ebook)
Subjects: LCSH: Akashic records.
Classification: LCC BF1045.A44 J44 2021 |
DDC 133.9--dc23
LC record available at https://lccn.loc
.gov/2020035002

ISBN 978-1-5072-1433-6
ISBN 978-1-5072-1434-3 (ebook)

CONTENTS

INTRODUCTION

Have you ever wondered if you've lived previous lives? Have you known how to perform tasks or spoken about information you have no previous experience with in this lifetime? Have you ever felt like you're here on Earth for a specific purpose but you don't know what it is? All of these questions can be answered through accessing the Akashic Records.

The Akashic Records are an energetic, vibrational record of everything that has ever happened in the past, present, and future. This includes actual events and words said during your human life, as well as thoughts, feelings, and intentions you've experienced. The Records also include moments from every past lifetime your soul has experienced on Earth and can even tell you about your future lives as well.

Accessing the Akashic Records can help you understand your true purpose in life. They can reveal your soul's journey and allow you to tap into past lives and incarnations to help heal issues in your current lifetime. Essentially, the Akashic Records will help you figure out who you are and where you came from. Perhaps you have an uncanny knowledge of herbs that can be used as medicine but have never studied this. It could be information from a previous lifetime when you were a doctor, herbalist, or healer. Maybe you have a specific fear, such as heights. It's possible you experienced trauma in a previous life where you or someone you love was hurt or killed in an event involving a high altitude. The good news is, when you discover stories and information from your past lives, it allows you to heal any issues that were carried over into your current lifetime.

That might sound like an overwhelming concept, but it's actually possible for anyone who puts their mind to it to access these records. All you need is an open mind and a willingness to learn. The word *Akasha* can be loosely translated from Sanskrit as "sky," "atmosphere," "space," or "aether." This translation helps explain how the Records actually exist on the astral plane, a nonphysical dimension that can be reached by setting an intention through meditation or by entering a trancelike state.

If this isn't your first foray into the world of spirituality, you might have already experienced the astral plane through astral projection, shadow work, or meeting your guides. These experiences have likely provided information that has helped you on your life's journey. This book will take your experiences and advance your journey even further. If you're a newcomer to this type of spirituality, this book will walk you through all the necessary steps to reach the Akashic Records. You will learn the spiritual basics—from meditation and using your third eye chakra to the many different ways humans can receive clairvoyant information—and become adept at getting into a relaxed state of being (and staying there), protecting yourself and your energy, and decoding the information you receive.

The Akashic Records can be a source of deep understanding about your soul's journey in this lifetime and others. If you're looking for spiritual guidance and a stronger connection with your soul, this spiritual pathway can illuminate the way to your inner truths. It's time to recognize and appreciate all that you are on a deeper level than you ever thought possible.

Part One

Getting Started

If you've never heard of the Akashic Records before, you may need to suspend your preconceived ideas about life, death, and how the universe works in order to understand what they are and eventually experience them. If you're a spiritual newbie, the very concept may at first sound impossible to you. Let go of everything you *thought* you knew about the universe; let's get into the details.

Chapter 1
Understanding the Akashic Records

If you are new to the concept of the Akashic Records, this chapter will give you a basic understanding of this expansive topic. You'll learn what the Akashic Records are and the many impressive ways that they can impact your life. You'll learn about the history of their existence, from early spiritual texts like the Bible...and even how they show up in modern pop culture.

THE AKASHIC RECORDS, DEFINED

The Akashic Records are an energetic, vibrational record of everything you think, do, and say—including from this, previous, and future lifetimes. It's like the entire universe is being recorded and stored inside a vast, cosmic "text" of sorts.

Are They in an Actual Book?

No, they are not literally in book form, but thinking of them that way is a helpful device we can use to ground this mind-blowing idea—that there's a record of every thought and experience the universe has ever had—in a concrete way. When your brain receives information it can't process, it pulls from examples that are familiar and that it recognizes from real life. We perceive this information as records or a book because we're used to finding information that way in our everyday lives.

To take it one step further, what you see during an Akashic Records reading is actually your subconscious mind's projection of what it thinks the Akashic Records might look like. For most, we imagine the Akashic Records housed in a library or hall-like setting. The Records themselves will usually appear to us like a book or even a series of books.

Understanding the Concept

Well, that's a lot to digest! The concept is not the easiest thing to wrap your head around at first—but don't feel intimidated. As you read this chapter and beyond, try to simply open your mind to ideas you might not have entertained before. We'll be discussing some deeply spiritual, cosmic, and mysterious topics. Some might be hard to believe at first while others might resonate with you immediately. Some people believe in things just by learning about them while others need to experience them firsthand in order to believe. Learning more about the Records will help you choose the path for accessing them that's right for you.

What's Included in the Records?

Much like the Internet, the amount of knowledge inside the Records is too vast to quantify and is constantly expanding. It includes every thought every person has ever had, every word ever spoken, and every life lived on planet Earth.

How Can Accessing the Records Help Me?

These records serve several important functions, such as:

- Helping you understand your true purpose in this life. If you're struggling to find meaning in your current job, situation, or life as a whole, accessing the Akashic Records can help you learn more about your past lives and what you're here in this lifetime to learn.

- Allowing you to tap into past lives and incarnations in order to help heal your current lifetime. Learning more about your previous lifetimes can help shine a light on why things are the way they are in your current life. We're here on this planet to learn lessons and advance ourselves spiritually, so the lessons you didn't learn in your previous lifetimes are the ones you're still trying to learn in this one. Learning about them now opens the possibility of avoiding the same mistakes you've made in the past, learning the lessons you need to learn, and healing yourself from the traumas of previous lifetimes.

- Showing you how to figure out who you are and where you came from. You're so much more than just [your name] from [your hometown]. The Akashic Records will show you what your purpose is in this lifetime so you can gain a much deeper understanding of your soul.

Through all these functions, working with the Akashic Records will help you live a much happier, more abundant, and more purposeful life.

Where Are the Records "Stored"?

When you access these records, you're actually retrieving information from a completely different dimension! This is because our lives on planet Earth are a three-dimensional way of living. Both scientists and spiritualists agree that there are many other dimensions beyond these three that humans don't currently have the capacity to comprehend. However, it won't necessarily feel like you've traveled into another dimension because your human brain and body simply aren't used to receiving these highly energetic codes of information.

Who Can Access These Records?

You'll be delighted to know that anyone is able to tap into this massive amount of information at any time. It is your divine right as a living being on this earth to access your records whenever you would like to. Don't let any spiritual teacher tell you you can't unless you have special powers because any soul who wants to further their knowledge can. This book will outline the steps to take to open up this field of knowledge to you.

It is your divine right as a living being on this earth to access your records whenever you would like to.

How to Access the Records

We'll discuss the many ways to tap into the Records throughout this book. In short, most people use meditation as a way to clear their mind so they can access them. Any kind of hypnotic or trancelike state will work, though. Other people even access it through prayer or energy healing, like Reiki. The Akashic Records can take some time and practice to reach, so keep practicing and don't give up. (Some spiritually advanced people can hop right into them whenever they'd like, but think of that as a long-term goal for now.)

No One Can See Your Records Without Your Permission

No one can gain admittance to another soul's records without their explicit permission—so no, there's no interdimensional spying going on. You don't need to worry about anyone else finding out the secrets in your life because they won't be granted access.

Some people also believe we are *always* accessing the Records through our higher self or clairvoyance. Could it be possible that those feelings you get in your gut are actually a message from your inner knowing or from knowing what's inside your Akashic Records? The answer is different for everyone, but after reading this book you may discover what *you* think.

THE AKASHIC RECORDS IN HISTORY

As previously mentioned, the word *Akashic* comes from the word *akasha*, which translates from Sanskrit into English as "sky," "atmosphere," "space," or "aether."

Akasha As an Element

In many religions and spiritual beliefs, Akasha is considered to be a fifth element (the original four elements being air, fire, water, and earth), an energetic field that connects everything in existence. This field is a dimension we don't see on the human plane. The ancient Egyptians understood this element—their pyramids reflect the five elements on their sides: earth, fire, water, and air on each visible side of the pyramid, with aether being represented by the bottom square that can't be seen by the human eye.

Ancient Greek Thought

Greek mythology included a deity named Aether, whose attributes included embodying the "upper sky," the purest of air that only the most powerful of gods would breathe.

References to
"The Book of Life" in Religious Texts

Throughout history, many civilizations refer to "The Book of Life" in their religious texts. For example, the following Bible verses all allude to the presence of a set of complete records:

- Luke 10:20 says, "Rejoice that your names are recorded in heaven."

- In Psalm 139, David mentions that in "thy book all my members were written," of which he says, "such knowledge is too wonderful for me."

- Revelations 20:12 makes a reference to "The Book of Life," saying, "Another book was opened, which is the book of life, and the dead were judged according to their works by what was written in the books."

- Christianity, Judaism, and other religions make reference to "The Book of Life," though it's not always defined in the same way.

Written References to the Records

As the people on this planet expanded their consciousness, they were able to tap into new spiritual learnings they hadn't yet been able to understand. The first mention of the Akashic Records in recent history came from Helena Petrovna Blavatsky, a Russian philosopher and author in the 1800s. In her 1877 book *Isis Unveiled*, she spoke of "indestructible tablets of the astral light" on which "is stamped the impression of every thought we think and every act we perform."

A few years later, in 1883, Alfred Percy Sinnett published *Esoteric Buddhism*, which cited Henry Steel Olcott's words on early Buddhism, saying they were "clearly held to a permanency of records in the Akasa, and the potential capacity of man to read the same when he was evolved to the stage of true individual enlightenment."

Rudolf Steiner, an Austrian philosopher and clairvoyant who lived from 1861 to 1925, spoke of what he called the "Akasha Record" often. He was known to be able to access the Records and used them as research tools to explore some of the unknowns around Christianity and the life of Jesus. His spiritual research became known as the "Fifth Gospel" since the information he spoke of exists outside of what is written in the Bible but some believe it to be historically accurate. In a 1913 lecture, he spoke about the insights he learned, saying that reading the Akashic Records is "very difficult and takes much effort to extract images" and that they are "very difficult to observe." Still, he mentioned that his process consisted of "clairvoyantly absorbing" the information while doing so.

THE AKASHIC RECORDS IN MODERN TIMES

Currently, the Akashic Records are still pretty under the radar in terms of widely shared religious and spiritual texts. However, they are growing in popularity. With the introduction of the Internet, we are able to share our spiritual discoveries, practices, and experiences much more easily with people the world over. New people discover the Records just by browsing the web. Additionally, people are more open-minded to such spiritual pursuits than ever before. That's probably why the Records—or unnamed versions of something very similar—have begun popping up in cultural expression.

The Records in Pop Culture

Nowadays, the Records appear sporadically in TV and film. For example, Benedict Cumberbatch and Tilda Swinton project into the astral dimension in 2016's *Doctor Strange*. (While you don't have to astral project to reach the Akashic Records, they are indeed located on the astral plane.) The two "timekeepers" in the movie separated from their bodies, traveled to the astral dimension, and had full conversations with each other while their human bodies were in another plane of existence. The astral plane is also where T'Challa goes when he speaks with his father, T'Chaka, in 2018's *Black Panther*.

In a 1999 episode of *Charmed* titled "They're Everywhere," Prue, Piper, and Phoebe meet a man who is being hunted by warlocks because he "found the Akashic Records" in the desert and the mind-reading warlocks are attempting to find the location of this incredible knowledge.

In 2004's *Illusion*, Kirk Douglas plays a Hollywood director nearing the end of his life. This film-within-a-film shows Douglas's character inside an old-timey movie theater (standing in as the home of the Akashic Records) with different periods of his son's life playing out on-screen.

Prince released a song on his 2001 album *The Rainbow Children* called "Family Name" that directly mentions the Akashic Records. The funky song starts with a robotic-sounding recording that says, "Welcome, you have just accessed the Akashic Records genetic information division."

SyFy's *Eureka* included many storylines in its first four seasons about "the artifact," an antenna for the Akashic Records that exists outside the space-time continuum. The "artifact" was kept underground in the town of Eureka and was only accessible by top researchers until—you guessed it—the bad guys got a hold of it.

When you think about it, the storytelling in ABC's *Lost* can easily be seen as an allegory for the Akashic Records. Each episode of the show generally focused on one character's flashbacks to different periods in their life. You could see how the flashes between the present—a bunch of spirits likely on the astral plane after a plane crash—and past of these characters effectively act as an all-knowing record of their lives.

The Future

It's a very exciting time to be living in as we constantly learn more about how to access the Akashic Records. And who knows what the future holds? Some day we might all be checking in with our records daily to help us make decisions and live our lives in a more comfortable way.

THE BASIC STEPS OF READING THE AKASHIC RECORDS

Over the course of this book, you'll learn exactly how to access the Akashic Records. The following is a short overview of the whole process so you know what to expect.

Step 1:
Prepare a Space and Remove Distractions

The first step in accessing the Akashic Records is to take stock of your personal surroundings in the place where you plan to have your session. You should ideally be in a quiet place with zero distractions because you'll be going into a meditative or trancelike state to access the Records. You'll want to remove anything that makes a loud noise or could bother you during this time. Tell your roommates or family members to leave you alone for a while so they don't interrupt your session.

Your comfort is important, too, as being too cold or uncomfortable can distract you from the goal at hand. You may decide to clear the energy of the room you're working in through sacred smudging or other energetic exercises. Set up the room with light music, incense, candles, or anything else that will put your mind at ease. You'll learn more about this step in Chapter 4.

Step 2:
Set an Intention

Next, you'll need to figure out what your goals are for the session. Goals can vary from person to person—you may be looking for major things like the true purpose of your life, or you might just want to access the Records to expand your spiritual consciousness. Any goal that feels right to you is absolutely perfect. Once you have a goal in mind, set an intention for the session that aligns with that goal. Then you'll need to figure out what questions you'd like to ask the Akashic Records. You can write them down or set them as an intention or mantra to repeat in your mind throughout the session. Remember that you want to ask questions that will give you as much information as possible, so it's smart to ask open-ended questions rather than those that can be answered with a simple yes or no. Setting intentions is the focus of Chapter 5.

Step 3:
Open Your Mind

In order to access the Akashic Records, you have to visit the astral plane. This means you'll need to work on strengthening and focusing your energetic vibrations. This can be achieved through meditation, energy healing, prayer, eating highly vibrational foods, and by doing energetic practices such as Reiki.

Most people use meditation to access the Records but any kind of hypnotic or trancelike state will be an ideal environment for the transmission. Others have been able to access it through prayer or energy healing, like Reiki. As mentioned earlier, some people believe we are always accessing the Records through our higher self or clairvoyance.

Goals can vary from person to person—you may be looking for major things like the true purpose of your life, or you might just want to access the Records to expand your spiritual consciousness.

The more you work with your third eye chakra and hone your clairvoyant abilities, the stronger your readings will be. We'll do a lot of work on these topics in Chapters 6–9.

Step 4:
Connect to the Akashic Records

Next, it's time to actually connect to the Akashic Records. You can do this by meditating on your own or by following a guided meditation designed specifically for the Akashic Records. (You can find many audio recordings for free on *YouTube* if you need inspiration.) You can also call on your spirit guides to help you connect with the Akashic Records as they will be happy to do so. If you're experienced spiritually, you may already have ideas on how to enter a trancelike state and can simply practice that way. (Some people use crystals during meditation to help calm them or to ignite their third eye chakra during a session.)

You can also work with a professional who is trained to guide people through Akashic readings. They can either talk you through each step of the process or, with your permission, communicate with the Records on your behalf. You'll learn how to access the Records and what will happen when you do in Chapters 10 and 11.

Step 5:
Ask Your Questions

Once your session has started, you'll eventually make your way to the Akashic Records while in your trancelike state. You may see the

Records visually as a hall or library, or you may see nothing at all. You might notice that your spirit guides are there with you. You may communicate with the spiritual guards who protect the Records or your guides may speak with them on your behalf. Sometimes you may not see or be asked anything at all. However, once you have access, it's time to ask your questions. You may speak them out loud or think them in your head—either way works. We'll discuss forming your questions in Chapter 5 and how to ask them in Chapter 11.

Step 6:
Listen for an Answer to Your Question

After you've asked your question, make sure you give ample time to listen for an answer. This is especially important if you plan to ask multiple questions as you don't want to fire them off one after the other and not leave time to receive a response. The method for receiving answers is different for everyone and will depend on which of your clairvoyant senses is the most developed. Some people will hear the answers spoken to them, others will see clear visuals of what they've asked, and some won't hear or see anything at all but will instead have a strong internal knowing of the answer.

While you want to be patient as you wait for an answer, you also don't want to wait forever since you may not receive an answer during your session. It's possible you'll come to understand your answer in the next few days, or it may appear to you in a dream. Chapter 11 will explain this topic in greater detail.

Step 7:
Evaluate the Information You Received

After your session has ended, it's important to take the time to record what you experienced in a journal. Sometimes the answers you get aren't necessarily what you were expecting or don't really make sense at the time. Write them down anyway. After multiple Akashic sessions, you may start to piece things together to form a bigger picture.

If you didn't receive any information during your session, it's a good idea to do some light troubleshooting to figure out why. It's possible you didn't get the information you seek because it's simply not the right time for you to learn it. Trust that the universe will provide the information you need at the right time. Chapter 12 offers even more ideas about how to try again if your first attempt didn't work as you expected.

MOVING FORWARD

Now that you're aware of what the process looks like in its entirety, it's time to learn more about the Akashic Records themselves. You'll want to keep an open mind, prepare your space the best you can, and enjoy the process of learning more about yourself and your soul's history.

Chapter 2

Discovering, Cleaning, and Protecting Your Energy

Everything in the universe carries its own energy and you are no different. Your energy is something you should be aware of and protect. This chapter will teach you about energy fields and how to cleanse yours when it encounters energy that doesn't serve you. You'll also learn how your energy can affect your experience with the Akashic Records. Accessing such a highly vibrational, cosmic text isn't easy for just anyone to do. Your personal frequency and vibration will need to be as clear and elevated as possible in order to make the connection.

UNDERSTANDING ENERGY

Did you know the human body has its own energetic field that extends far beyond its skin? Everything you see, smell, touch, taste, and think is actually composed of energetic vibrations. That includes you, your family, your friends, your pets, your home, your meals, your possessions...everything! Your energetic field, also known as an aura, extends two to three feet outside the body. (It can be extended even farther to fill up a space if you'd like it to.)

In broader terms, this means that what you perceive in this world as being physical or material isn't that at all. Matter is an illusion of light and energy. The idea that everything on this earth is not exactly what it has traditionally seemed to be is, at first, radical, but when we turn to science, both Albert Einstein's findings in the previous century and current studies of quantum physics confirm this theory.

Energy Makes Up All Matter

Let's get into the scientific weeds for a moment. Quantum physics is the study of how atoms, energy, and the universe work at a cellular level. It is the study of the particles that make up everything in existence—including humans. Ultimately, quantum physics has proven that solid matter doesn't actually exist on Earth.

In science class, we learned that atoms are made up of protons, neutrons, and electrons. Protons and neutrons can be further divided into quarks, which are the smallest particles known to exist. Quantum physicists have shown that what's inside protons, neutrons, electrons, and quarks is nothing more than energy, perhaps even energy vortexes not unlike the seven chakras.

Working from smallest to largest, particles form atoms, atoms form molecules, and molecules form physical matter. This proves that everything on Earth is actually made of energy, not solid matter. It may seem like the objects you hold in your hand are solid, but quantum physics proves otherwise.

Albert Einstein famously published his theory of special relativity in 1905, in which he wrote the equally famous equation $E = mc^2$. What this equation means is "energy equals mass multiplied by the speed of light, squared." In layperson terms, it shows that mass and energy are interchangeable—essentially the same thing but in different forms. It also explains that mass increases relative to how fast an object is moving through the universe. Quantum physics later proved this to be correct, demonstrating once again that Einstein was a true genius.

YOUR PERSONAL ENERGY FIELD

Like everything else, humans are energetic beings. We are all born with the ability to sense energy, though most of us lose these skills because we don't cultivate them. Still, some memory of them remains. That's how you're able to sense when the energy is off when you walk into a room or when someone is keeping their true feelings inside while maintaining a happy front on the outside. That sensation is a form of clairvoyance, a term meaning "intuitively reading energy." When you tune into the energy of places, things, and those around you, you can pick up all sorts of information you wouldn't have had otherwise. What does this mean for your everyday life? Well, first, you should consider checking in on and taking care of your personal energy often.

When you tune into
the energy of places,
things, and those around
you, you can pick up
all sorts of information
you wouldn't have had
otherwise.

How Your Energy Impacts Others

We are energetic receptors and must cleanse our personal energy of the outside energy with which it comes into contact. Since everything is energy, you should think about the energy you're putting out into the world and how it could affect others. If everything is energy, we must consider the energy that our own actions put out into the world each and every day. The words you say, the feelings you feel, even the thoughts you think have much more power than we give them credit for. We are all operating on different frequencies, and only you can decide if that's a high vibrational frequency or a low one. Do you want to be a beacon of light in this world, emanating positive energy to everyone you meet, or do you want to spread your bad vibes around, keeping your power small while infecting others with your negativity? The choice is yours.

Others' Energy Affects Yours

The opposite is true as well—outside energy can impact your own. Have you ever felt the presence of someone who walks into a room as soon as they enter, good or bad? Whether they meant to or not, their energetic field commanded the attention of your space and might have even given you a clue as to that person's mood or emotions.

Another reason to be conscious of your energy field is all the places you drag it through every day! If you live in a big city, your aura is moving through the auras of potentially hundreds of other people's energetic fields in a single day. Why does that matter? Because you might absorb or be influenced by their energy. When someone edges into your personal space on the subway, it's not just their close physical proximity that affects you—the other person's energy could also change how you feel. Sometimes others' energy can make you feel worse. For example, have you ever walked into a room filled with downtrodden people and found yourself immediately feeling blue? On the other hand, other people's energy can uplift you, like when you celebrate the big win of a team you root for and find yourself feeding off the excitement of everyone else around you.

Both of these are examples of being influenced by the energy fields of others. It's something that happens without a thought. This tends not to be a problem if you find yourself reaping the benefits of living or working with positive, effervescent people, but if you're going to an office every day where workers are yelled at and treated like garbage, that will absolutely have a negative impact on your energy. If you've experienced trauma of some sort in a specific place, going back there will likely trigger an emotional response from you because you're reacting to the energy of that place. (If it's a location in your own home, you can take steps to clear the energy and start fresh. If it's not, avoid the place entirely if you can. If you can't, this book will teach you how to go in with your energy protected and ready to go.)

Your Energy As Your "Battery"

Another way to look at the way energy impacts you is by comparing your energy to a battery. Think of a product that might use, for example, a AA battery—remote control, children's toy, etc.—and how the performance of that item deteriorates as the battery begins to die. You find yourself pushing harder on the buttons of your remote control, making sure it's pointed right at the TV receiver and smacking it with your hand to make it work. The toy robotic dog that usually scurries around the house starts moving more slowly until the "woof woof" noises it makes sound more like "waaaaarrf waaaaarrf." However, when you take a moment to replace their batteries, both items spring back to life and operate as if you'd just bought them.

Cleansing your energy and taking steps to protect it will recharge your "battery," leaving you powered up and ready to take on the world.

You and your energy operate the same way. Day after day, unpleasant influences on your energy take a toll on your physical health, mental health, and personal life. Cleansing your energy and taking steps to protect it will recharge your "battery," leaving you powered up and ready to take on the world.

ENERGY AS CHAKRAS

A chakra is a spinning wheel of light or an energy vortex located in key spots around your body. The energy within them is constantly spinning and regulating the energy flow within you. The human energy field is made up of many chakras, but most studies focus on the main seven:

1. The crown chakra (located at the crown of your head)
2. The third eye chakra (located between your eyebrows)
3. The throat chakra (located toward the bottom of your throat)
4. The heart chakra (located at the center of your chest)
5. The solar plexus chakra (located approximately two inches above the navel)
6. The sacral plexus chakra (located approximately two inches below the navel)
7. The root chakra (located at your perineum)

Each of these chakra centers is associated with a different color of the rainbow and each monitors a different part of your energy flow.

- The crown chakra is violet (sometimes white) and represents spirituality and your connection to the Divine.

- The third eye chakra is indigo and represents your intuition, wisdom, vision, and awareness.

- The throat chakra is blue and is connected to communication and your voice.

- The heart chakra is green (sometimes pink) and has to do with all matters of the heart: love, forgiveness, and overall healing.

- The solar plexus chakra is yellow, representing your personal power source.

- The sacral plexus chakra is orange and controls your creativity, inspiration, and sexuality.

- The root chakra is red (sometimes black) and represents the most basic sense of safety and security in your life.

If the energy in any of your chakras is blocked, it can lead to issues directly related to the chakra in question. For example, your solar plexus chakra is your power center. When its energy is blocked, you will struggle with self-confidence and insecurities. You will learn much more about using the chakras to access the Akashic Records in Chapter 10.

HOW TO CLEAR YOUR ENERGY

There are many different methods of clearing your energy so it is no longer contaminated by anyone else's. This can be a simple process or an ornate ceremony, whichever you prefer. This section will outline a variety of ways to clear your energy. Some options can be combined or simply used on their own as is.

Smudging

Smudging is an ancient form of cleansing that uses herbs to cleanse yourself or an area. To smudge a space, you'll need your smudging herb of choice, a fireproof ashtray or equivalent container to catch the falling pieces, and a match or flame to light it. Herbs you can smudge with include sage, palo santo, cedarwood, sweetgrass, mugwort, frankincense, myrrh, rosemary, and bay leaves. The most commonly used is white sage, known for its cleansing properties. Once you have your materials, follow these steps:

1. To really get your cleansing started right, you can set an intention specific to cleansing your energy.
2. With your lit candle or match, light the herb in the ashtray or container.

More on Purchasing Herbs

The recent rise in popularity of smudging has led to a shortage of certain herbs because more and more nonindigenous people are purchasing them, so use them wisely. I also strongly recommend purchasing your herbs from local sources and native peoples whenever you can.

Grounding

Another easy way to clear your energy is to visualize sending it into the ground. Our planet has its own vibrations it is constantly emitting, and this energy is very pure and cleansing. When you send your vibrations into the Earth, the planet cleanses it for you. When you visualize replacing the energy you just expelled with the Earth's energy, it's believed it cleans out and refreshes your energetic system. This can be accomplished easily through various visualizations. For example, you can envision:

- Sending all your energy through the bottom of your feet into the Earth's core. While you can do this anywhere—from the top floor of a skyscraper to an airplane in mid-flight—you might enjoy greater results by doing this barefoot outside in the grass, sand, or other outdoorsy area.

- Roots growing from your feet all the way to the Earth's core and sending your energy into the ground. This is especially powerful if you're sitting with your feet on the ground.

- Pulling the Earth's energy up through roots that grow from your feet.

No matter how you do it, enjoying the feeling of the Earth's grounding energy will help you clear your own.

Breathing Exercises

Breathing is an excellent way to clear your energy because it keeps energy moving inside your body. When we breathe deeply, fresh oxygen breaks up energy blockages and refreshes our system. If you have a breathing exercise you already love, you may be able to use or modify it to help cleanse your energy as well. If not, the following is a quick and easy exercise to make it happen.

1. Take a deep breath and inhale as much air as you possibly can. As you do so, envision light filling your body.
2. Release the air inside you as fully as you possibly can, either by exhaling loudly, quickly, or as robustly as possible. As this happens, imagine yourself breathing out old or negative energy.
3. Repeat steps 1 and 2 until you feel better.

You can also breathe in a pattern by counting numbers. An easy way to do this is to take a deep breath for four counts, hold it for four counts, breathe out for four counts, then repeat the whole process until you feel better. There are many techniques that require breathing for a different number of counts, so feel free to try a few options until you find one that resonates. You could also consider using other visuals, such as imagining your lungs are balloons and that you're filling them up with each breath. Experiment until you find some visuals that work for you.

Take an Epsom Salt Bath

Who doesn't love a relaxing bath at the end of a long day? Did you know you can turn your bath into an energy-refreshing experience with the addition of Epsom salts? These magnesium-friendly salts can help relax your muscles, detoxify you, ground you, and cleanse your energy all at once. If you don't have a bathtub in your home, you can achieve similar results by putting your feet in a bucket filled with warm water and Epsom salts. As you bathe, visualize your energy being cleansed by the water or the ground (via the salts).

Visualizations

There are many types of visualizations you can use to clear your energy. Visualizations are one of the easiest ways to clear your own energy because all it takes is a little imagination. This means you can do it easily in almost any location and time frame—while on the train to work, in a doctor's waiting room, or standing in line at the grocery store. You may even choose to make them a ritual in your everyday life. When creating these visualizations, the more specific you can get, the better; when envisioning a cleansing light, you must absorb it with every fiber of your body and every single cell inside every single fiber. You can imagine light washing over your body, being zapped by a lightning-like energy, taking an energy shower, or any other method of cleansing you enjoy. Try out the following visualizations:

- **Egg of white light:** The most well-known and popular visualization is the egg of white light, and with good reason. The human energetic field is in the shape of an egg surrounding the body, so all you have to do is envision a big egg surrounding your body and fill it with the brightest, whitest light you can think of. This will help you cleanse your aura.

- **Shower of golden light:** This method is as simple as it is beautiful. This visualization requires you to stand, sit, or lie down and picture a stream of bright, sparkling gold light above your body. As you stand, sit, or lie there, envision cleansing beams hitting every part of your body. You can say a prayer or mantra at the same time, or you can just imagine this shower.

- **Violet flame:** Also known as the "Holy Violet Flame" or "7th Ray," the violet flame is a very powerful visualization. All you do is request that your guides and/or the universe wash you with a violet flame light. (Note: Violet flame healing can be intense, so have a drink of water afterward and, if you're feeling lightheaded, try grounding to recenter yourself.) Here are some ways to do that:

  - You can envision actual violet flames "burning" away any energy that doesn't serve you and isn't completely clear.
  - You can imagine a shower of violet flames above your head that takes away stale energy.
  - You can picture waves of violet light "zapping" away the unwanted energy each time they hit your body.
  - You can simply imagine violet light washing over every inch of your body, from head to toe.

Mantras

Mantras are simply sounds, words, or phrases that are repeated over and over again to aid in concentration and/or meditation. They originated from Hinduism and Buddhism, but you may have experienced using a mantra in other spiritual studies as well. You may even have some mantras at the ready for different situations in your life. If not, this section will help you come up with the perfect mantra for you.

The most important parts of a mantra are that it's easy to remember and that the message is important to you, otherwise you might not stick to the practice of repeating it. For an energy-clearing mantra, you'll want to make sure whatever you come up with has a commanding nature to it. The intention to refill your energy, clear your energy, or avoid absorbing the energies of others should be a major part of it. If you need help starting out, the following are some simple options that should yield positive results right away:

- "My energy is clear."
- "Their energy is not mine."
- "I cleanse my body with light."
- "I am filled with light and love."
- "I am an egg of bright white light."
- "I do not absorb the energy of others."
- "My aura is cleansed and clear."
- "I radiate positive energy."
- "My energy is thriving."
- "I am the violet flame."
- "I am cleansed."
- "I am light."

HOW TO PROTECT YOUR ENERGY

After you've cleared your own energy and are feeling fresh-faced and ready to take on the world, you don't want it to be depleted immediately upon walking out the door. The following are some practices to keep up your energy levels all day long.

Egg of White Light

As stated earlier in this chapter, envisioning an egg of white light around your body is an excellent choice for energy work because it's the same shape as the average human's energy field. To use this egg of white light to protect your energy once it's been cleansed, visualize the egg with the brightest white or golden light radiating from within and without. You can do this at any time or call upon it regularly as a daily ritual. Some people do this every morning when they step outside their door while others use it whenever they know they're going to be in a busy public place with lots of people. Many others don't have a specific daily ritual for this practice and choose to keep it in their spiritual toolbox for when they feel it's needed.

Using Crystals

Crystals have many great uses in the spiritual realm but protecting your energy is one of their most powerful. They're extra convenient as you can easily wear crystals as jewelry or fit a small stone in your pocket or bag. Pocket crystals are an extremely popular form of crystal for this very reason. These stones are very easy to find for purchase and are generally about an inch or two in size. For the most part, these stones have been tumbled so they're smooth, making them an ideal shape to put anywhere. You could place a grounding stone like red jasper, hematite, or garnet in each pocket to help you stay composed throughout the day and feel, well, grounded. Amethyst is known to be an extremely soothing and calming stone, making it a popular choice.

While it can feel extremely balancing to walk around with a stone in each of your pants pockets, you don't have to keep the stones in your actual pockets. Some people put them in their jackets, purses, or even in their bras (just make sure they're secure enough so they don't fall out of your shirt). Note that you don't need to use two crystals for this; one stone will absolutely work. On the other hand, you can also fill up your pockets with as many stones as you'd like! You may want to experiment with how the stones actually feel in your pockets and whether or not you want to be reminded of their presence throughout the day.

You don't need to physically wear the stones to receive their benefits, either. Many mineral-lovers have stones throughout their homes: an amethyst at the doorway, selenite or a bowl of rubies by the nightstand, and a salt crystal as a night light. You might find that placing a crystal, like pyrite or citrine, by your desk helps you to focus better on the work in front of you. Many people use crystals to help improve their sleep by either placing stones underneath their pillows, next to their nightstands, or underneath their beds. Selenite, angelite, smoky quartz, and amethyst are all terrific choices for this use.

Crystals have many great uses in the spiritual realm but protecting your energy is one of their most powerful.

Cleansing Crystals Before Using

It is important to both spend time with a new crystal once you've purchased it and to cleanse the stone often. If you've tried working with a gemstone and found it didn't resonate with you, you may have forgotten to cleanse and program the stone upon bringing it home. The first step of purchasing a new crystal is always to cleanse its energy. You can do this by smudging it with sage or another sacred herb (for more information on smudging, see the section earlier in this chapter), placing it on a clear quartz or amethyst stone, or by using your intention to clear the old energy out of it. You can cleanse many crystals by running them under or soaking them in water, but you must first make sure the crystal isn't too soft on the Mohs scale of hardness to handle it.

Finding Your Crystals

If you aren't sure what types of crystals are for you, there are many books available that will explain the healing properties of each and every stone. There are thousands of varieties of crystals and you could spend months pursuing texts written about them. An easier way to select stones that resonate with you is to enter a shop that sells a variety of stones. If a certain stone "jumps out" at you or catches your attention, it's likely a stone that will be of service to you. If you're a little more advanced and can sense the vibrations coming from stones, you'll be best off letting your hands guide you.

If you want to focus your crystal use on energetic protection, start with stones that are black, red, or dark in color as they tend to have protective qualities and often correlate with your root chakra, which grounds you to the Earth. Here are some great stones to start with:

- Black Tourmaline
- Smoky Quartz
- Garnet
- Hematite
- Shungite
- Onyx
- Red Jasper
- Tiger's Eye

Keep in mind that you should clear these stones before using them as darker stones tend to pick up and accumulate old energies.

Whether you believe in the metaphysical properties of healing crystals or not, they are at the very least a reminder to keep up your energy that you can keep on your body. In that sense, carrying a talisman or other item that is special or feels lucky to you can achieve similar results.

Body Language and Position

Another way to seal off your energy is to use your body itself, either by moving it or using certain poses to protect certain parts of your energetic field. For example, if you're in a room where someone is glaring at you from across the way, you can adjust your position so you don't see them anymore. Even better, you could remove yourself from the room entirely. If you're in the middle of a conversation with a negative person or energetic vampire (a person who sucks the energy from others, whether they realize it or not), you can fold your arms in front of your chest to protect your heart (and heart chakra) from the energy they are sending your way.

Visualize Protection Around You

This is a very powerful way to keep yourself protected, and it can be personalized in a manner that works for you. Essentially, you call on your guides, angels (such as the Archangel Michael), or loved ones on the other side to protect you, then simply envision them surrounding you.

How they surround you is completely up to your imagination: They can envelop you in a circle, they can be sending their light down from the sky, or they can be standing right next to you as if they were about to battle your enemies like in a superhero movie. Whatever makes you feel like you have spiritual backup will work!

Envisioning a Beam of White Light

One of my favorite ways to protect my energy is by using rays of white light. This can be used in any situation but is especially powerful when you know ahead of time that your energy could be affected by something. For example, if you know in advance you have a really intense meeting scheduled by your boss, you don't have to let their stress command all the presence in the room! Instead, you can actively project beams of white light from your body from the moment you enter the meeting room until the moment you leave. If you know you need to have a conversation with someone who is down in the dumps, you can beam your light directly onto them so it essentially overpowers their dread. You might even discover your beams of light can change the attitude of the other person or even a whole room full of people!

Chapter 3
Connecting to Your Soul

———

To fully comprehend the Akashic Records and their spiritual ties, there are three concepts we'll need to explore further. This chapter will take you through them all. The first is the law of attraction, which essentially states that you will bring into your life whatever you are focused on. Next, we'll discuss reincarnation and its ties to the Akashic Records. Finally, we'll discuss the purpose of your life on this earth and how an Akashic reading can help clarify it for you.

WHAT IS THE LAW OF ATTRACTION?

The law of attraction states that energy attracts like energy, meaning you attract things into your life that match your vibrational frequency (which can be high, low, or anywhere in between). The law of attraction doesn't mean you'll immediately obtain something or someone just because you're hoping and praying for it; it means your thoughts, actions, emotions, and overall vibrational frequency will attract things of that same nature into your life. In theory, it's not about what you want; it's about being grateful for and happy with what you have, which will in turn attract more of those blessings into your life.

Like Attracts Like

The law of attraction also influences the types of people you bring into your life. Oftentimes, we're attracted to people (whether in a romantic or platonic way) because they share qualities similar to those we see in ourselves. These qualities are also energetic frequencies, and your energy is finding a match in another person's energy.

Similarly, you may find people with a vibration that's different than yours to be off-putting. You may sense that you should stay far away from a person or you might pick up on a vibe that's ill-intentioned. This can happen when dealing with people whose vibrations are very low and their energy dense or dark. But don't be too quick to judge—after all, you've surely at one point in your life been in a terrible mood for one reason or another. While in a bad mood, if a person walks in who's all smiles and beaming high vibrational light, you probably want them to go away immediately. Neither one of you is better than the other; your vibrational frequencies simply don't match at that moment.

How to Raise Your Vibration

Those who follow the law of attraction generally try to maintain a higher state of energetic vibration. The idea is to raise your vibration as high as it can go so you attract things of a similar vibration into your life. How do you achieve this? Here are some ideas:

- Take time for spiritual practice (such as accessing the Akashic Records).

- Cleanse your energy regularly.

- Adjust your outlook on life: Negative thoughts are actually negative energy, so you'll want to find a method of moving away from them.

- "Clean up" your social habits. Gossip, being rude, and speaking ill of others (or yourself) can all lower your vibration.

The law of attraction is powerful because it can help you strive to be the best version of yourself in order to attract the things you desire in this lifetime.

The Law of Attraction and the Akashic Records

The law of attraction relates to the Akashic Records because they are both highly vibrational energies. When your frequency is vibrating at its highest rate, you attract things into your life that match the same frequency. Since the Akashic Records are highly vibrational, you can access them more easily (and potentially for longer) if your frequency is high as well.

The law of attraction is powerful because it can help you strive to be the best version of yourself in order to attract the things you desire in this lifetime.

REINCARNATION—YOUR SOUL'S LONG HISTORY

Another spiritual concept that ties into the Akashic Records is reincarnation. Reincarnation is the idea that your soul has lived multiple lifetimes before its current one and will continue to live other lifetimes after this one. This concept boils down to the idea that we are all souls living in human bodies who have decided to live on this earth at this time for a specific reason.

Most of us are familiar with the idea of a soul. It's the spirit or essence of a person, the part of us that is immortal and never truly dies. It is widely believed in many religions around the world that when one dies, their soul lives on. Reincarnation takes things one step further by suggesting that our soul or spirit has probably lived many other lives on this planet before and that we may come back to this planet in another lifetime after we die. We then return to the spiritual realm to reunite with our loved ones who have crossed over and assist those we love who are still on Earth.

Reincarnation Etymology

The word *reincarnation* is derived from "carnate" (flesh), "incarnation" (soul or spirit entering the body), and "re-" (happening over and over again).

In general, people do not recall their former incarnations without actively seeking out knowledge of them. You can do so through past life regressions, an Akashic Records reading, and other spiritual quests.

However, you may have seen an example of someone—usually a child—who spoke of their past lives on a talk show. These intuitive children are born with or stumble upon the knowledge of their previous lives because, as we've discussed, children are innately receptive to the spiritual realm, energy, and their own clairvoyance. Such examples should not be dismissed as they can make a profound case for reincarnation's existence.

Reincarnation also has ties to karma. Karma is the spiritual principle of cause and effect, meaning the intentions you have and the actions you take in this lifetime will influence your life directly. In essence, you reap what you sow. Oftentimes a soul will come to Earth to make amends for karma in a past life. Of course, you as a human being don't actually know this information upon birth and you'll have to go through your life learning lessons and healing those karmic ties. Many spiritual teachers believe we have known most of the people we meet in this lifetime in other lifetimes. Regardless, each person you meet is a chance to build a better, more positive experience than you might have had in your last life.

Many spiritual teachers believe we have known most of the people we meet in this lifetime in other lifetimes.

DISCOVERING YOUR SOUL'S PURPOSE

Reincarnation suggests that souls choose to incarnate on this planet at a specific time because they have unfinished business of sorts, unresolved issues from a previous lifetime. Some souls come to learn lessons; some come to observe the current state of affairs; others come to help other souls, either specific souls or the general population; and some come just to enjoy being in a physical body.

Your soul knows what you need to learn or solve in this lifetime, even if you aren't consciously aware of it yet. Tapping into the Akashic Records can help you decipher what your soul's purpose is—you just have to ask.

One thing is clear, though: Material gains are never your soul's purpose. Society has conditioned us to desire things like becoming wealthy and powerful or running a *Fortune* 500 company. Maybe you've accomplished some of these material wins in your own life. You'll know, then, that these types of accomplishments do nothing to serve your soul. There are many stories of wealthy, power-hungry people who achieve all their goals only to still feel empty inside. That's because these types of wins are usually self-serving.

What Is Your Purpose?

Discovering your soul's purpose is important work. Your soul's purpose will no doubt have to do with creating joy, growing spiritually, and/or assisting others on their journeys. If you're considering what your purpose could be, take a look at your life.

- What brings you the most joy?

- How do you bring joy to others?

- What are your strengths?

- What comes naturally to you?

- What fills your heart with happiness?

- What have you taught others?

- What gives you the feeling that you are making the world a better place?

  Odds are that these answers will help show you where your true purpose lies.

Finding your purpose
can be a journey that
takes your entire
lifetime.

Be Patient

Finding your purpose can be a journey that takes your entire lifetime. There is no rush to discover what yours is. You may have already asked the universe but haven't gotten a clear answer. This may be because you aren't yet ready to understand it fully. It may also mean that you must discover the answer for yourself, through a series of practices and lessons learned during your lifetime. Divine timing is always right, so don't be frustrated if you haven't figured out your purpose just yet. You will.

You'll think more about your soul's purpose in Chapter 5 as you set intentions for your Akashic Records session. For now, simply contemplate these concepts as you begin to prepare your mind and body to access the Records.

Part Two

Getting Yourself Ready

Now that you better understand what the Akashic Records are, it's time to get into the details of how to access them. Unfortunately, you cannot just shout a question up to the skies and receive an answer. It requires getting into the right mindset, being open to receiving answers, considering what you aim to get out of the process, and a bit of preparation. This portion of the book will begin to take you through that process.

Chapter 4

Preparing Your Physical Space

Even though the Records exist in another plane, you'll want to consider the space around you to make sure it's conducive to clearing your mind. This chapter will give you lots of easy ideas for transforming a space in your home into a comfortable, welcoming, and spiritually charged site for accessing the Records.

BLOCK OFF DEDICATED TIME

The first thing you'll need to do as you seek out the Records is set aside some uninterrupted time for your session. At first, you'll need at least forty-five minutes to an hour. (After you have a few sessions under your belt, you may decide to shorten them.) This step is important because it's incredibly frustrating to be in the middle of a session only to find yourself distracted or interrupted.

If you have young children in the house, you're likely better off practicing after they go to bed or before they wake up. You can access the Records at any time, day or night, so the timing is really up to you; just make sure you're clear of known distractions.

If you're using an audio meditation to guide you through your session, check how long it is to make sure you're free for that entire length of time.

FIND A SUITABLE LOCATION

To choose a location for your Akashic Records transmission, you don't need to worry about clearing out a whole room. If you have a meditation corner or altar, you may have already laid out the perfect spot. Otherwise, all you really need is a comfortable spot without distractions. You can be inside or outside—just find someplace private where you'll be able to relax and focus on yourself.

ELIMINATE OR MINIMIZE DISTRACTIONS

Now that you know when you'll have time for your session, get rid of the distractions in the room you're working in.

Cell Phones

Your phone is probably the most distracting item you have to deal with. Start by switching your phone to the silent setting or airplane mode. Cell phones can distract you in so many ways—texts arriving, alarms going off, phone calls coming through, notifications beeping—that it's best to put the phone out of sight, even in another room if possible. If you need it for music or a guided meditation, make sure you've turned off all your alerts and dimmed the screen as much as possible.

Other Devices

It's not just your phone that's begging to take your attention away from the task at hand. Doorbells, alarm clocks, computers, printers, dishwashers, and laundry machines can all make bothersome noises that you might normally ignore. If you're especially new to meditation or silent concentration, you'd do well to take an inventory of your chosen room to see if there are other things that could easily annoy you. For example, you might have a clock with a second hand that ticks quite loudly or a fan that makes noises as it swivels from left to right. If you get the sense that these will truly bother you, it's best to move them into another room to achieve peace.

Interruptions

Another thing to think about are people who could interrupt you. If you live with a spouse, family, or roommates, you should consider where they will be at the time of your session. If they're home, it might be best to do this alone in your bedroom. Place a sign on the door asking not to be disturbed unless there's an emergency. If you have a shared bedroom, you might ask your roommate about a time they won't be around and try it then. If you have young children in the house, remember that you should have figured out a time to do this while they're asleep.

Even if you live alone, there is still an array of interruptions that might surprise you: a neighbor stopping by to say hello, the doorbell ringing with an unexpected delivery, etc. If these things happen to you frequently, you might consider placing a sign on your front door requesting that people not ring the bell. These types of interruptions happen, of course, so try not to get too frustrated. Just focus on minimizing the distractions within your control as best you can.

CREATING A SENSE OF PEACE IN YOUR SPACE

Now it's time to make your space as comfortable as possible.

Items and Décor to Consider

Although accessing the Akashic Records requires no extra tools beyond your brain, you do want to be as peaceful as possible during your session, so making sure your space is pleasant is well worth the time and effort. You don't need to purchase anything fancy—items you already own will work fine. Here are some ideas of what to use:

- A yoga mat to lie down on
- Meditation (or regular) pillows to sit on
- A blanket to lie down on

Let There Be Light

Don't forget to consider the lighting in your space. While natural light is best, lamps are particularly helpful in the corners of rooms where energy can become stagnant. Placing a lamp in a space that hasn't been cleared or attended to in some time can rid the area of old energy.

The Temperature of the Room

Your best bet is to keep the space at room temperature so you aren't too hot or too cold. If your room is likely to be cold, keep a blanket beside you in case you start to feel chilly during the session. If your space tends to get warm, you might want to layer your clothing so you can remove something if you get hot.

The Room's Scent

It may seem like a silly thing, but the way a room smells can really affect your concentration and sense of calm. To start, are you going to be near anything that could smell bad? Being too close to the bathroom, trash, or dirty laundry can distract those with a sensitive sense of smell. If you're in a space that needs a little improvement, you might want to supplement it with another scent, particularly one that's relaxing to you. Here are some options:

- Fresh-cut flowers or herbs.

- Candles, particularly the nontoxic and soy-based variety, can be an excellent choice. They fill the air with a lovely scent, set the mood, and bring the element of fire close by.

- Essential oils—such as lavender, rose, or sage—can be burned or diffused.

- Incense is another favored method of aromatherapy, and you can find many combinations of scents.

You may also choose to smudge the area with sage or another traditional herb before you begin. (We'll dive much deeper into smudging later in this chapter.)

If you choose to burn anything, it's important to make sure there's a fireproof tray underneath it to catch any embers that may fall. Since you'll be in a trancelike state, the last thing you'll want to be worrying about or noticing is your room catching on fire—safety first!

POSITIONING YOUR BODY

Now that you've organized your space, you can think about choosing a position you'll be comfortable in for your session.

Lying Down

One option is to lie down on your back, either in bed or on a couch. You'll need to decide how many pillows you'd like, if you want blankets to lie on, and if you want a blanket on top of you or beside you. It's worth lying down for a quick moment before beginning to see if the setup is actually comfortable. If it is, you'll be in the ideal spot for your session.

One thing to note when you lie down is you might find yourself falling asleep given the right conditions: too late at night, being too comfortable, or being too tired or exhausted in general. If this happens, know that you may still receive messages while asleep and/or as dreams. You may even wake up with the answers you asked for, so if you drift off, all is not lost!

Sitting Down

Another option is to simply sit down. There are a couple of ways to do that:

- Sit upright in a chair or on a couch with your feet planted firmly on the floor and your back pressed against the back of the chair or couch.

- Sit on the floor, either with your legs crossed or positioned comfortably on a cushion. This is the way it was done in ancient times, often with specific hand positions (mudras) or movements.

Generally, if you like sitting down to meditate or relax, this will be a good option for you. You'll still want to try out the space you've decided on before you begin. You may also need a blanket and/or pillows on a chair or couch, so be sure to have them ready.

OTHER DETAILS

Try to take note of any other random circumstances you might be able to address beforehand. For example, if you have a cold, make sure you drink some tea, grab some tissues, or take some medicine or supplements to alleviate your symptoms. If you tend to get thirsty, keep a cup of water within arm's reach. If you frequently use the bathroom, make sure to go right before you start.

Whatever your "thing" is, don't shame yourself! The idea here is not to shine a light on life's annoyances or faults but simply to create an optimal experience that meets your every need.

HOW TO CLEAR A SPACE VIA SMUDGING

When practicing any spiritual tradition, including accessing the Akashic Records, it's always a good idea to clear the location's energy if you're able. Smudging, the practice of purifying a space with sacred smoke and herbs, will clear your space of stagnant or negative energies before you begin your Akashic Records work. Researchers are even looking into whether smudging can actually change the molecular structure of air and/or clear airborne bacteria! Spiritually, clearing a space cleanses the energy of anything that doesn't serve you, paving the way for light and positive energy to enter. With regular space clearing, your home will feel warm, inviting, and be a great place to do some spiritual work.

Spiritually, clearing
a space cleanses the
energy of anything that
doesn't serve you, paving
the way for light and
positive energy to enter.

A Brief History of Smudging

The practice of smudging has been used all over the world for many centuries. Here are some examples:

- Some Native American cultures use white sage and other herbs while performing extremely sacred rituals.

- Tribes in South and Central America used copal, a tree sap, to smudge.

- The Incans used palo santo in ceremonies.

- Ancient Egyptians and ancient Greeks are believed to have used frankincense and myrrh—two of the three gifts said to have been bestowed upon Jesus in the Bible—to smudge.

- Indigenous Australians used emu bush leaves.

Many indigenous cultures and families from these regions still use these sacred herbs. Because these sacred herbs have cultural meaning, make sure you source them ethically and/or locally.

Decluttering

Something else to consider when identifying a space for spiritual work is all the items you have inside it. Keep in mind that every single thing in your home has its own energetic vibration. Is your home cluttered with old items that have bad energy? If so, a smudging ceremony can only do so much. It will clear the air in a space but it cannot clear every item in your home. You may want to smudge individual items to take care of this. Conversely, you may want to get rid of many of these items. You can also clean up the area, putting items into boxes so they're out of the way.

VARIOUS HERB CHOICES

All of the aforementioned herbs can be used for smudging and, while they all achieve the goal of clearing a space, each herb has different metaphysical properties to them. Use the one most closely related to your needs:

- **White sage**, currently the most popular and widely available smudging herb, is known to get rid of negative energy, cleanse your aura, connect with your intuition, and clear a space of unwanted energetic beings or spirits.

- **Palo santo**, which means "sacred wood," clears a room of negative energy and fills it with positive energy. This makes it a great companion for white sage in that you can cleanse a room of negative energy first with sage, then use palo santo to fill the room with positive energy.

- **Sweetgrass** is a highly sacred herb to Native Americans. Like palo santo, it is often used after sage. It can be used to cleanse a room of negative energy and bring in positive energy. Unlike some of the other herbs discussed, it is quite thin (it is grass, after all) and is braided together before drying. It is often burned for smudging purposes but can also be worn as an amulet or placed in a specific area for good luck or to ward off bad vibes. It has a vanilla-like scent combined with the smell of fresh-cut grass or hay.

- **Frankincense resin** has been burned since ancient times and is believed to have powerful protective energies that can clear a space. Spiritually, it is used to cleanse an area before a ritual is performed because it calls in angels, spirit guides, and other positive light beings to oversee the space. Frankincense is associated with the third eye chakra and is said to cleanse that chakra and aid with intuition. It's highly vibrational, meaning it sets up your space for deep spiritual learning and/or communication. Its properties are also considered to be antiseptic, which means it could clear your space of airborne germs.

- **Cedar** is used to expel negative energy and invite good energy. It is often used to cleanse a new home because of its inviting properties. Cedar can be burned as a dried piece of wood or as its foliage, bundled up like a stick of sage.

- **Juniper** can be similarly bundled up for burning and its berries can be burned as well. Juniper has both cleansing and protective properties and is said to help bring success.

- **Pine needles** can be burned separately or bundled. They have cleansing, healing, and cleaning properties.

- **Balsam fir** smudges are calming and relaxing and smell like a typical Christmas tree.

- **Mugwort** cleanses negativity from a space and brings a sense of calm to it. Also called "dream weed," it is known to stimulate dreams and aid in lucid dreaming. Some place mugwort underneath their pillow for protection during slumber. Try using it at night to see how it impacts your dreams. Mugwort can also be used to literally sweep away negative energy from a space when used as or incorporated into a broom.

Flowers and floral-smelling plants can be used for smudging, too, such as these:

- **Lavender** is known to bring peace and happiness to a space and can reduce negative emotions or energies. It has calming properties as well.

- **Rose** petals or dried roses are also very calming. They can be used to clear energy and invite love into any room. Roses, in particular, have a scent that lingers long past being burned, so make sure you enjoy how they smell.

DIY Smudging Bundles

To make your own smudging bundles or sticks at home, you'll first need to plant or purchase whatever tree, herb, or flower you'd like to make them from. Once it's grown to the necessary length, follow these steps:

1. Cut off 8"–10" pieces of the branches.

2. Cut a thin string or cord to a length that's 4–5 times as long as the branches you've cut.

3. Pick up the branches and hold them in a bouquet-like arrangement.

4. Turn the "bouquet" upside down and tightly tie the string at the top, where the stems are.

5. Wrap the string around the bundle again and again, moving from top to bottom, until you reach the end of the string. Make sure you leave a few inches of string to tie together at the bottom of the bundle.

6. Set the smudge stick to dry for a week or two (or as long as it takes to dry completely).

Specific Home-Cleansing Rituals

Following is a simple, go-to smudging exercise to clear the energies of your personal space. You'll need:

- Your bundle of herbs (representing the element of earth)

- A match or something to light the herbs with (representing the element of fire)

- At least one open window or door so the cleared energy has somewhere to go (otherwise, you're essentially just moving the energies from room to room and aren't actually cleansing the space)

- A fireproof bowl to catch ashes (representing the element of water—even though there's no water—because it's a bowl)

- A fan, feather, or even just your hand to help spread the smoke around (representing the element of air)

If you conduct this ritual regularly, you may decide to create an altar or special box to keep all your tools in one sacred place.

Alternatives to Smudging

If you live in a space that doesn't allow an open flame or you feel discomfort at the idea of burning things in your home, there are alternatives to traditional smudging you can turn to. One example is using an essential oil diffuser. You can fill these with any combination of sacred herbs that have been distilled into an oil and use them to smudge. Another option is to use a room-clearing spray, also made with essential oils. This option works well because you can spray the oils directly into the spaces you want to clear, whereas a diffuser is usually stationary.

Once you collect your materials, you're ready to begin.

1. Focus your thoughts on inviting clean, positive energy into your space.

2. Light your smudge stick with a candle or flame with the same focused thoughts.

3. Once lit, begin to move your smudge stick slowly around your space. It's tradition to move in a clockwise motion throughout a space, but you may not have a home that's conducive to that, so do the best you can. (You may choose to smudge your body first.)

4. As you walk through each room, focus on each movement you make, intending to rid each room of any negative or stagnant energy. You may want to repeat a mantra or saying while doing so. Make sure you're also walking into the corners of each room as you do this.

5. Upon finishing, tradition states the rest of the herb should be returned outside, and once it is no longer burning, either scatter onto or bury into the ground.

Now that you've cleansed your space, you want to make sure you fill it with positive energy. You can accomplish this by using another herb that brings in positive energy like sweetgrass, palo santo, or cedar. You can also use a room spray or you may choose to bring in fresh-cut flowers or herbs.

HOW TO CLEAR A SPACE USING CRYSTALS

You can also use crystals to cleanse a space. When using crystals for space clearing, you must first make sure the stones themselves are cleansed. You can achieve this by smudging them, running them under water, or laying them out overnight underneath the Moon. You can then program the crystals to act as cleansing agents simply by holding them in your hand with that intention in mind. Here are some crystals to consider using:

- **Selenite** is a powerful stone that doesn't need to be cleared but can be charged. It's great to place along the perimeter of your home, above doorways, or in each corner of a room.

- **Rose quartz** is a stone that brings love into your home and is great to place either as large pieces or smaller pieces inside a bowl.

- **Black tourmaline** can absorb unwanted energies quickly but needs to be cleansed every so often.

- **Amethyst** is excellent at clearing away anxious or nervous energy.

- **Black obsidian** can be placed in your doorway to absorb negative energy before it even enters your home.

HOW TO CLEAR A SPACE USING SOUND

You can use sound to clear a space as well. For any of these options, focus your attention on cleansing the space to ready it for spiritual work. Following are sound-based energy-clearing ideas:

- **Ting sha bells**, a set of metal bells traditionally used in Tibet, have been used for ceremonial acts and to change the energy of a room for hundreds (if not thousands) of years. If you can't come by these particular bells, any set of bells will do. Ringing bells throughout your home will release sound vibrations that can cause unwanted energies to immediately disperse.

- **Singing bowls** are another excellent way to use sound to clear energy. Singing bowls are standing bells shaped like bowls that make a specific sound when hit with a mallet. Each bowl has a specific vibration, which helps you de-stress by balancing your chakras and cleansing the cells of your body. Buddhist monks have used Tibetan singing bowls in meditation for centuries.

- **Drums** have been used throughout history to perform rituals, and using them to clear a space works just as well. Any type of drum will work for space clearing. All you need to do is bang on your drum throughout the area you want to cleanse.

- **Clapping** your hands is another way to move stagnant energy in a room. Clap along the perimeter and in the corners of the space you want to cleanse.

In all of these instances, make sure your instruments are being played throughout the space, stopping in each corner along the way.

Using Sea Salt

Another method of clearing a space is to place a bowl of sea salt in it. It's believed the salt will draw in and absorb bad energy, so make sure you toss the water outside within a few days of placing it out. You can also use a salt lamp, which is said to release negative ions into a room. Negative ions have a relaxing effect on the body by increasing levels of seratonin.

MAINTAINING YOUR SPACE

Preparing your space can take a bit of time but it's well worth the effort. You've just created a quiet, comfortable, safe, and energetically clear space for your journey ahead. Maintaining this environment doesn't take a lot of work—an occasional decluttering and smudging will keep your space looking and feeling inviting. And now that your external space is ready, you can begin some internal work.

Chapter 5
Setting Intentions

In all aspects of life, from starting out on a new adventure to chipping away at a long-held goal, setting an intention can help focus your energy in a productive place. That's why you'll want to set a direct intention for the work you plan to do to access and obtain information from the Akashic Records. In this chapter, we'll discuss what intentions are, who you'll meet along the way, and what you could see during an Akashic Records reading.

WHAT IS AN INTENTION?

In a general sense, an intention is a plan or decision to act. An intention in the spiritual sense is a bit more super-charged. Spiritual intentions symbolize the start of every goal, dream, or creative endeavor. Setting a spiritual intention is the process of focusing your consciousness on a goal you wish to achieve. This process activates your energy field, raises your vibration, and tunes your vibrational frequency into your intention, thus drawing it toward you. In other words, setting an intention jump-starts your spiritual gears and kicks your plan into motion.

Intentions vs. Goals

Setting an intention is a bit different than setting a regular goal. Goals represent your immediate desires, while intentions are larger plans that will set you on a path for life. For example, you might really desire a new product that's just come on the market. Unless this item will revolutionize your life in some way, getting it is probably a regular goal.

FIGURING OUT YOUR INTENTIONS

Intentions relate to a much bigger vision of your life than goals do.

To start creating intentions, take some time to think about what you envision the rest of your life to be like. To awaken your curiosity and wonder, consider these questions:

- What do you want to accomplish?
- How will you nourish your soul?
- How do you want to feel at the end of your life?
- What is your soul's purpose?
- Are you searching for a sense of purpose?
- Are you feeling lost?
- Do you suffer from an illness or disease?
- Are you seeking more professionally?
- Do you feel lonely?
- Have you been impacted by a death that you'd like to come to terms with?
- Do you crave a change in your life but don't know why?
- Are you considering a major life change?
- Has your world been rocked by a surprise recently?

These larger questions may be difficult to wrestle with, so try to instead frame them as amazing opportunities to create the life you truly want rather than letting your life "happen" while you watch. Plus, when you have a clear idea of what you want, you'll be able to set meaningful intentions that will pave the way for your larger goals to come true. If you're still unsure about what you're seeking after spending time with these deep questions, asking about your life's purpose in an Akashic reading could give you the answers you're looking for.

USING YOUR INTENTIONS TO CREATE A QUESTION SPECIFIC TO THE AKASHIC RECORDS

Once you've given some thought to the direction you want your life to go in, you've probably encountered a topic or two where you could use some guidance. That's where the Akashic Records come in! An easy way to come up with a question to ask during your Akashic Records session is to consider your intentions and walk back from there.

If your intention is to expand your spiritual consciousness, you may ask to be enlightened with information that will serve you in this lifetime. If your intention is to discover your passion in life, you can ask, "What is my soul's true passion?" or "How can I bring more passion into my life?" If your intention is to learn more about your past lives, you can simply ask, "What lessons from my previous lives would be beneficial to know in my current life?"

An easy way to come up with a question to ask during your Akashic Records session is to consider your intentions and walk back from there.

Methods of Brainstorming

To decide on the intention for your Akashic Records session, it is best to spend some dedicated time thinking about what you want to achieve in your reading. You should set aside some time to sit alone with your thoughts in a format that works for you, such as:

- Writing down your thoughts or questions in a journal

- Meditating on it

- Sitting in front of a computer with a blank note open and brainstorming

- Drawing pictures or making a "mind map" where you freewrite topics and connect similar ideas or topics with lines and/or circles

Really, any method of thinking hard about a subject that works for you will help narrow down your intentions.

If you still aren't sure where to begin—or aren't entirely sure about the whole experience—you could start by asking to confirm the Akashic Records themselves. You could say something along the lines of "Allow me to experience the Akashic Records firsthand" with the intention of learning about and/or seeing the Records for yourself. You'll be surprised at the information that can come through and the lessons you'll learn just by inquiring about the Records themselves.

Narrowing It Down

After you brainstorm, try to narrow it down to one question per session. The pure enormousness of the source at hand can make that difficult to do, however! How do you ask only one question of an all-knowing source containing every event that's ever happened in the universe so far, not to mention what will happen in the future? Unfortunately, you're not going to walk away with every answer to your and everyone else's problems in one session. In fact, it's much more beneficial (and productive) to focus on one question per session. This is because the information at hand is in another dimension, encoded in a language that our brains need to translate in order to have it make sense to us. If you rapid-fire your queries all at once, it won't leave enough time for you to process the information you're getting. It may also confuse the guides who guard the Akashic Records (but more on that later).

Finding Lessons in Any Experience

In times of distress, you may not be able to look at your life in such a grandiose way or see that far ahead. In times like these, you may want to ask, "Why is this happening to me?" However, you may not get a clear answer. Oftentimes, learning important life lessons comes from hardships that simply must be experienced. You might try asking, "What lessons am I to learn from this moment in my life?" or "What can I learn from past lives to help me through what I'm going through now?"

If you are really struggling to determine which question to ask first, here are some ideas:

- Hold a meditation session where you think about each of the questions you have in mind and see which one feels the most stirring to you.

- Pray on it.

- Ask the universe what you should ask and stay still to listen for an answer.

- Ask a close friend for advice (though keep in mind their answer will likely be a projection of the questions they seek the answers to in their own lives).

- Work with a pendulum to see which question will help you on your journey the most.

If these options fail, take a more structured approach and write all your questions down, then rank them in a numbered list and start with your first question in your first session, your second in your second session, and so on.

CHOOSE YOUR WORDING

The actual words you use in your intention are important. Words are extremely powerful, and some people believe that every word you put into the universe sets that reality into motion—so you must choose your words carefully. Others believe words don't matter as much as your intention does. Either way, don't be careless with your word choices as you formulate your intention. Think back to a time when you fought with someone you're close to. Their words could hurt, right? Sometimes they can cause pain physically, like a metaphysical gut punch. If negative words can hurt, it must stand to reason that positive words can create happiness. Make sure your intentions are pure and spoken with kindness.

For example, you may have someone at work you don't get along with. You wouldn't intend to "take them down and get their job" because that's entirely negative (and not a great perspective to have in general). Instead, you could ask to advance your career or take the next step in your job. Another example is that saying "I want to stop feeling lonely" isn't as strong as "I want to meet new people and expand my social horizons." Take some time to reflect on your intentions. If negative ones keep coming to you, try writing them down and converting them into something positive.

Words are extremely powerful, and some people believe that every word you put into the universe sets that reality into motion—so you must choose your words carefully.

PREPARING TO SET AN INTENTION

When you set intentions, you are officially announcing your desires to the universe. To formally set an intention, you'll want to first clear your mind. Deep breathing exercises, meditation, mantras, and/or prayer will help put you in the right headspace. Clearing your mind helps you focus on nothing else but your intention as you set it. There is no one right way to set your intention, but here are some suggestions:

- Speak it out loud.

- Repeat it like a mantra, either aloud or silently.

- Pray with it in mind.

- Call on your spirit guides and tell them about it.

- Write it down in a journal or even just on a piece of paper that you'll carry with you or place in a special spot.

The process of formally setting your intention is a great way to keep yourself focused during your Akashic Records session.

KEEPING TRACK OF YOUR INTENTIONS

Writing down the goals you've set for yourself is extremely helpful in tracking your progress with any new hobby or activity. In the case of the Akashic Records, writing your goals helps to reinforce the intentions you've set, keeps them at the top of your mind, and allows you to celebrate your progress along the way. You may decide to write your intentions down in a journal or on a piece of paper. Others repeat their intentions in their mind like a mantra. You could also choose to not write it down at all (though it helps to remember!) if your memory is solid. Regardless, you'll want to keep this intention or goal in mind during your session, however you see fit to do so.

Chapter 6
Clearing Your Mind

In these modern times, we've become a society that is always on the go. For many of us, it's hard to actually stop our metaphorical wheels from spinning long enough to catch our breath. Our bodies are oftentimes caught in fight-or-flight mode, a stress response from our hormones that keeps our nervous system working in overdrive because it believes we're in danger. It's designed to work only in short bursts when we're in *actual* danger. When our bodies are put in this state regularly, it can deplete our adrenal energy and compromise our immune system.

Unless you live in the middle of nowhere, you're likely experiencing a constant barrage of stimuli, not to mention that we're constantly connected to our screens, whether phone, computer, or TV. These distractions prevent our brains from focusing on the task at hand and can keep us in a stimulated state. If it's difficult to imagine being able to relax your mind long enough to have an Akashic reading for any of these reasons, this chapter will offer ways to calm it down.

DEEP BREATHING EXERCISES

Tuning into your breath cycle is a powerful way to help eliminate stress and get into a Zen-like state. Taking deep, slow breaths has a cleansing effect on your mind *and* body. It's also entirely free, which means it's accessible to everyone—plus, it can be done at any time. It doesn't require any special equipment or training either, just a few simple patterns to remember. Continued practice of deep breathing exercises can change the way your body reacts to stress; studies have shown that regular use of breathing exercises can help to rewire the circuits in the brain to respond less drastically to daily stress.

General Breathing Techniques

Deep breathing exercises are generally quite simple. The goal is to breathe slowly and as deeply as you can while focusing only on the act of breathing. To do this:

1. Find a comfortable spot to sit or lie down.
2. Close your eyes and slowly inhale through your nose or mouth. You should be able to feel your body filling up with air until it can't take in any more.
3. At this point, you can choose to hold the breath in for a bit longer or to immediately breathe it out slowly, doing so until it feels as though there's not a single bit of air left inside your body.
4. Once all the air is out, you may choose to hold the breath out for a moment, or you may jump back to inhalation.
5. Repeat steps 2–4 until you begin to feel less stressed.

When you breathe, make sure you're using your diaphragm—not just filling up your lungs—so you take in as much air as possible. This is called diaphragmatic breathing or taking a "belly breath." Performers and classically trained singers are taught about this early on, but not everyone understands that the breathing cycle uses much more of the body than just your lungs.

The human breath begins in the nose or mouth and then moves downward to the diaphragm. When the diaphragm contracts, it signals the lungs to expand and take in air. During exhalation, the diaphragm relaxes and essentially pushes the air out of your lungs. Breathing "into your stomach" helps to visualize the true breathing pattern and will encourage deeper breaths.

Be Sure to Concentrate

Concentration is key to relaxing while breathing. Try to really focus on how it feels to bring fresh air in and push old air out. Here are some ideas on how to keep your focus on belly breathing:

- Place your hands on your stomach and watch them rise and fall with each breath.

- Keep your mind from wandering by focusing on one single thing, for example, the exact place where the air meets your skin—your nose. Feeling the way the air hits that one place can be deeply relaxing.

- Visualize taking in bright, light energy with every inhalation and exhaling dark, stale energy. A great mantra to repeat during this is "I release all that no longer serves me."

- Think of your favorite color filling every inch of your body with each breath. This color can be visualized as waves of energy swirling around your body, cleansing it with every inhalation.

- Imagine you're in a place you find relaxing. An example would be to imagine yourself lying on a beach, watching the waves roll in as the Sun kisses your skin. Your mind will begin to relax in this imagined environment, allowing you to focus on deep breathing.

- Focus on each part of your body in order, either from your toes up or your head down. With this practice, you'll focus on each body part for a moment to release the stress in that area. You can visualize it being cleared with your breath, or you can actually tighten up the muscles in each area for a moment before relaxing them completely. Once you finish one area, move to the next. One option is to start with your toes, then move up to the following areas: feet, shins, thighs, butt, stomach, chest, fingers, arms, shoulders, neck, head. You can find guided meditations online that will take you through this process as well.

CONTROLLED BREATHING EXERCISES

Kicking deep breathing up a notch, controlled breathing adds the technique of counting breaths as you go. This rhythmic breathing technique includes counting how long you inhale and exhale, which gives your brain something to focus on. Controlled breathing helps promote relaxation by keeping chatter and thoughts from entering your mind. Typically, these techniques require counting a sequence of numbers in your head: breathing in for a certain count, holding the air in for a certain count, exhaling for a certain count, and sometimes holding a count while there's no air left in your system.

Controlled Breathing Takes Getting Used To

You may find when you start controlled breathing that you feel faint at first. This could be because you simply aren't used to breathing on a "schedule." It could also mean your body isn't used to taking such deep breaths. Regardless, this will occur less and less often the more you practice these breathing exercises. If it doesn't, you might consider talking to a doctor.

Controlled breathing helps promote relaxation by keeping chatter and thoughts from entering your mind.

The easiest method of controlled breathing is counting to eight. This technique is painless to recall—unlike some other methods—as you're just counting from one to eight over and over again. To try this method, begin by breathing in through your nose for eight counts. From there, hold your breath for another eight counts. Then release the air through your nose (or mouth if the nose is too difficult at first) for eight counts. Finally, count to eight again with no air in your body at all. Repeat for at least eight full breaths, if not more.

There are also variations on controlling exactly how you breathe in or out. Here are some choices:

- Breathing in and out through the nose is hugely popular in meditation.

- Breathe in through your nose and exhale through your mouth (or try the opposite) and see how it feels.

- Try nostril breathing, which requires you to hold one nostril down with your finger as you breathe in through one side and exhale through the other.

There are tons of combinations here, and you can play around with them to see what suits you best.

RELAX WITH AROMATHERAPY

Using your sense of smell to induce relaxation can be extremely rewarding. For one, there's not much to it besides inhaling and exhaling—what could be easier? It's also quite easy to obtain sources of these scents, whether it's using fresh-cut flowers, lighting a scented candle, setting up a diffuser, or burning dried herbs. Following are some ways to bring the power of scent into your space to relax you.

Candles

The most popular form of aromatherapy in Western civilization is probably scented candles. They come in every scent you can imagine and in a range of size, shape, and color. Read the label showing what the candle is made of before you buy it. The best candles for spiritual work are made from pure, all-natural ingredients that you've heard of before. If you look at the list of ingredients on one and don't recognize a single word, it's likely it's filled with chemicals that might not be the best to inhale.

Soy wax is a great alternative to standard candles, which are made with paraffin. Paraffin candles are made with chemicals you might not want dispersed in your home. Soy wax, on the other hand, is a sustainable alternative that produces much less soot than paraffin candles do.

The best candles for spiritual work are made from pure, all-natural ingredients that you've heard of before.

Essential Oils

Essential oils are pure, concentrated oils that are distilled or extracted from plants. They're considered to be volatile oils, which means they evaporate quickly and should be treated with care. Keep them in a cool, dry place and always make sure the cap is screwed on tightly. When it comes to essential oils, you can obtain the benefits of aromatherapy either by inhalation or using them topically. If choosing to use oils on your skin—for example, during a massage—make sure they're of the highest therapeutic grade. Most oils are mixed with a carrier oil like coconut, jojoba, or other vegetable oils to help your skin absorb it without drying out or causing any kind of reaction. They're generally sold separately, and you'll have to mix these in yourself. When using an oil on your skin for the first time, make sure to try a small drop first to see how your skin reacts before slathering it all over your body.

Some essential oils that work well for aromatherapy are lavender, sage, peppermint, eucalyptus, frankincense, and citrus oils such as lemon, orange, grapefruit, and bergamot.

Incense

Incense, on the other hand, is a natural, scented material that is burned directly so its smoke can waft around a room. Incense is made up of plants, herbs, essential oils, and powders. It comes in a variety of shapes—cones, sticks, coils, papers, ropes—and can also come as powders, pastes, or resins. The name comes from the Latin word *incendere*, which means "to burn," and it's been used for thousands of years, including by the ancient Egyptians, Babylonians, and throughout Asia.

To use most types of incense, you only need a flame and a fireproof container for the incense so it can burn safely. To use a resin-based incense, you'll need to place it on top of a hot coal for it to burn.

Smudging

While many use smudging to cleanse an area, person, or object (as discussed in Chapter 4), it can also be done simply for the smell. You can easily make your own smudging materials by purchasing dried herbs or by drying them out in your own home. Once they're dry, wrap string around a bundle of them and hang them upside down before lighting with a match or candle. As with any flame, use caution and keep the burning herbs in a fireproof ashtray or bowl for safety.

For relaxation smudging, try using roses, cedar, sage, lavender, balsam fir, sweetgrass, sage, or palo santo.

OTHER METHODS OF RELAXATION

There are, of course, many other ways to feel more relaxed. Any activity you enjoy and can fully immerse yourself in can empty your mind of nagging thoughts and clear your energy. For example:

- **Dancing and exercise** release endorphins and rid you of any jitters you may have.

- **Stretching your muscles** is a wonderful way to release tension and relax, as long as you fully concentrate on bending and how your muscles feel with each stretch. Yoga is also great for this.

"Earthing"—aka walking on grass or the bare earth with bare feet—is said to increase your connection with nature and help you obtain the Earth's energy.

- **Practicing pranayama yoga** focuses entirely on breath retention and respiratory control, combining deep breathing exercises with yogic movements. *Prana* means "breath" and *ayama* means "control," thus making the practice all about controlling your breath.

- **Singing, playing an instrument, or even listening to music** can also help you relax. Singing a song at the top of your lungs can be a great way to release stress, while playing an instrument requires concentration that will let you transcend into the music itself. Listening to music can be extremely therapeutic and can help to let out energy and emotions, but be aware of the genre you're listening to. If it's a song that triggers your emotions in a bad way (anger, sadness, etc.), listening to it could make you more stressed out than when you started. Stick to songs that pump you up, make you happy, or bliss you out and you'll be golden.

- **Spending time in nature** has been scientifically proven to promote relaxation. Taking a hike in the woods, spending a day at the beach, swimming in the ocean, or just lying in the grass in your backyard can all help you achieve a Zen-like state. Grounding techniques tend to be even more effective in nature and can be combined with visualizations to achieve peace. "Earthing"—aka walking on grass or the bare earth with bare feet—is said to increase your connection with nature and help you obtain the Earth's energy.

- **Getting acupuncture** helps your body holistically clear your energy systems for optimal performance. While sticking needles into your skin may seem counterintuitive to relaxing, the placement of the needles in specific places can actually clear energy blockages. Acupuncturists work along the meridians of your body, which are the paths that energy, or "qi," takes. Many people find acupuncture immediately relaxing—some even fall asleep on the table during a session—and repeated sessions can lead to long-term stress relief.

- **Tapping, aka E.F.T. (the Emotional Freedom Technique)**, offers a series of places on your body to touch to help train it to calm down. The process of physically tapping on specific energy points on the body can help to restore balance to your nervous system and relieve stress.

- **Treating yourself to Reiki treatments** can clear your chakras of any distress. Reiki energy works similarly to acupuncture in that it clears energy from our bodies but does so with human touch instead of needles. Though most Reiki sessions focus on the main chakra points, energy travels to whatever parts of the body need cleansing the most. Reiki has been compared to taking an energy shower or bath because of its ability to cleanse the entire body of stagnant energy quickly and with little discomfort.

- **Meditating** can train your mind to be ready for any stress that comes your way.

If all else fails or you sense that your inability to relax is out of your control, it might be a good idea to see a professional health expert in order to get to the root of the issue.

Part Three

Maximizing Your Spiritual Connections

The next step in your Akashic Records journey is opening your mind to different spiritual paths and teachings that will help you. For example, we'll take a look at clairvoyance, or psychic sight, and the different ways in which you can train yourself to pick up on extrasensory information. Studying the human chakra system will allow you to quickly identify areas in need of healing and to tune in more easily to your own energy. Embracing these spiritual principles will assist your advancement in accessing the Akashic Records, no doubt, but they may also leave you with a greater understanding of yourself too.

Chapter 7
Developing the Four "Clairs"

———

It may be hard to believe at first, but all of us have clairvoyant abilities. It may be dormant in you at the moment but that doesn't mean it's not there. Or maybe you're completely connected to your abilities and have honed them over the years. Or perhaps you're somewhere in the middle: You predict things that end up happening, you see visions now and then, or you have some sort of "knowing" inside but have never really thought about why. These "gut feelings" are usually more than just your conscience. No matter where you land on the psychic spectrum, there are things you can do to strengthen your psychic connection. In this chapter, we'll discuss the four main "clairs" of clairvoyance and how they relate to you.

THE BIG PICTURE: BE MINDFUL

One of the ways to help improve your connection to the spiritual realm is to practice mindfulness. When you aren't worrying about the past or future, you're able to fully reside in the present—that's mindfulness. We are all born with this mindset and clairvoyant abilities. It's often said that children are quite psychic because they haven't felt society's judgment about it and they don't doubt their gift. Most kids don't yet have the worries and fears that average adults do, enabling them to live in the present moment. They automatically live the mindful lives that so many adults come to realize they've been missing.

Communicating with the Other Side

While this book isn't about connecting with spirits on the other side, that can be something you tune into with your psychic abilities. Children very often see spirits and things that others cannot since they are mindful and in touch with their clairvoyant abilities.

CLAIRVOYANCE

Clairvoyance loosely translates to "clear seeing" and refers to your intuitive sight. It is also referred to as psychic sight. Clairvoyance, the most well known of the clairs, is essentially seeing things with your *other* eye—your third eye chakra. Seeing things in your mind's eye is an ability that everyone has but not everyone knows about or engages with. For example, if when you read a book you imagine what the setting and characters look like in your mind, that's another type of "seeing" in action. When you read "the sun shines down onto the glistening waves of a deserted beach as boats and seagulls pass by," do you see sparkling water, a quiet sandy beach, and some boats or seagulls? If you do, you're already on your way to harnessing your inner vision!

Clairvoyance is interesting in that it's an ability we all have yet we all process in different ways. Most people will see their psychic visions playing out in their head in the same way your imagination produces images in your mind. This can sometimes make it hard to decipher if you're getting a psychic message or if your imagination is running crazy, but with practice and spiritual work you'll eventually be able to tell the difference.

Seeing things in your mind's eye is an ability that everyone has but not everyone knows about or engages with.

Projecting Psychic Images

Psychics, particularly those who communicate with spirits, are often trained to project the visions they get onto an imaginary "screen" in front of them. This allows for messages to come in a bit clearer and be better organized. This method is most helpful when doing readings but isn't really necessary for everyday life. Some people are born with these abilities firing away and don't need to learn how to decipher intuitions or put their messages onto a screen. While that is a gift, it can sometimes feel like an overwhelming flow of intuitive thoughts, so it can be helpful to set boundaries as to when you want to access this information.

CLAIRSENTIENCE

Clairsentience is the ability to feel intuitively. You know the feeling when you arrive somewhere and something just seems "off"? Or when a friend is talking to you through a smile but you can tell that inside they're feeling deeply upset? These are both examples of clairsentience, which can also be described as reading the energy and vibrations of a person, place, or thing. Another instance of this is when you walk into a room after a heated argument has taken place. If you can feel the emotions and energy of what occurred in there, you're clairsentient.

You may even feel the energy of all the things around you, noting whether they feel light and airy, dense and heavy, or uncomfortable. Lean into this knowledge and, if something doesn't feel exactly right to you, follow your gut and avoid it.

Another example of clairsentience is how you react while watching the news. Do you often find yourself feeling upset or anxious while watching an upsetting news story? Do your emotions change from one piece of news to the next? You could be tapping into both the emotions of the collective consciousness and your own clairsentient emotions. This also goes for watching movies and TV shows and reading books. Clairsentient people find themselves deeply connecting to the characters they watch or read about: championing their wins, crying at their losses, getting excited when they go through something new. In fact, to practice your clairsentient abilities, try watching a movie or reading a book and really invest yourself in a character. Feel what they feel. Cry when they cry. Laugh when they laugh. Not only will this make you more empathetic; you'll also be working on your psychic abilities.

Clairsentience can also lead you to pick up on another's physical traumas. You may discover you know about a broken bone or a disease in someone's body before they tell you about it. This ability can serve you well as you monitor your own health. Many clairsentients know they're getting sick in the very early stages of an illness or even beforehand. They can also easily pinpoint parts of their body that need energetic healing and may find themselves drawn to energy healing work because of that.

Energy workers are often clairsentient. While doing their work, be it acupuncture, Reiki, or another type of energy healing, they can actually feel the emotions of whoever they're working on. With enough practice, they (and you!) can tune into the feelings of each chakra and give detailed feedback on the emotions tied to each one. Energy workers also make great massage or physical therapists because they can sometimes identify the source of pain even before the patient does.

Clairsentient people find themselves deeply connecting to the characters they watch or read about: championing their wins, crying at their losses, getting excited when they go through something new.

Clairsentience is extremely common among empaths—people who are extremely sensitive to both their own and others' emotions. They tend to have their energy drained very easily by others and can feel the emotions of those around them, usually without trying, easily becoming stressed by this deluge of feelings. If you relate to this, I encourage you to use the energetic protection methods discussed in Chapter 2 to help you cope.

What Is Clairempathy?

Clairempathy (also known as intuitive empathy) is the ability to immediately pick up on the feelings and energy of others. It is very similar to clairsentience but includes the ability to physically feel the energy instead of just sensing it.

CLAIRAUDIENCE

Clairaudience is the ability to hear things in your mind. Similar to the way you "see" with clairvoyance, instead of hearing through your ears as per usual, you'll "hear" things mentally. Have you ever asked your spirit guides, angels, God, or the universe a question and heard an answer in your head? That's clairaudience! You can communicate with your higher self or the Akashic Records in this way. Just center yourself, relax, and let the communication flow.

This intuitive hearing can come across in a number of ways, such as:

- **Hearing other voices speak to you.** You can talk to anyone, including your guides, loved ones on the other side, the universe, or even yourself. It's important that your mind is quiet enough to really listen for and receive the message.

- **Hearing your own voice speak to you.** Don't worry, this is totally normal—after all, most of us have an inner monologue running in our heads all day long that sounds like our own voice.

- **Hearing music.** Sometimes you may hear music that isn't being played by anyone at all. This happens especially in a psychic reading, when a spirit on the other side wants to send a message through song. It is sometimes difficult for those on the other side to speak or produce full sentences for us, so it can be easier to send a sound or song.

- **Hearing ringing in your ears or highly vibrational pitches.** It's said that these are communications from higher vibrational beings that humans cannot hear in a traditional sense. You may also pick up on different frequencies. For example, you might be able to hear that the TV or radio is on in a room on the other side of the house. This is a perfect example of clairaudience.

CLAIRCOGNIZANCE

Have you ever known the answer to something but didn't know how you knew it? That's claircognizance in action. Claircognizance is intuitive knowing or having a clear knowledge of something you haven't studied or learned before. It's when random knowledge pops into your mind about the present or future. For example, you may find yourself discussing with a friend or colleague something about their life when you blurt out something. Their face may turn pale or be utterly surprised, and they'll ask, "How in the world did you know that?!" This is your deep inner knowledge accessing information that even your friend might not know.

Spirit guides often use claircognizance to help you on your life's journey. Sometimes they may find it necessary to implant certain knowledge in you because it will serve you in a particular way. Other times, when communicating with spirit guides or asking them for advice, you may find you don't hear an answer but you suddenly know the answer. You may also get downloads of information while you're sleeping or in a dream. All of these are examples of knowledge being imparted to you.

In order to practice this skill, you'll want to work on your solar plexus and sacral chakras through meditation, energy clearing, and learning to trust your own power. It also helps to be in a relaxed state. Have you ever noticed that some people get their best ideas in the shower or right before drifting off to sleep? This is because your mind is at rest, which allows it to be in a receptive state. If you're having trouble honing this ability, you might try some activities where your body is working and your brain is not—anything that's automatic in nature or a little mundane. You could go for a drive, wash dishes, clean the house, run around the neighborhood, etc. As always, meditation is a great tool for this as well.

THE OTHER CLAIRS

Now that we've addressed the four main clairs, we should talk about the less common ones.

- **Clairalience** is the ability to smell intuitively. This is essentially being able to smell things that no one else can smell. Common scents picked up by clairalience are flowers, cookies, smoke, perfume, cigarettes, and other burning smells. Sometimes spirits will use the sense of smell during a psychic reading in relation to something that was special to them. There have even been stories about psychics who can "smell death" (but would you really want to know?).

- **Clairgustance** is the ability to taste things intuitively. This means being able to taste things that aren't there. This can happen when you're eating something but it tastes like something entirely differ-ent. It can also happen when you aren't eating anything at all and you suddenly taste something in your mouth. Luckily, this doesn't occur too often because, as you might imagine, it can be startling and/or unpleasant. No one really wants undesired tastes in their mouth.

- **Clairtangency** is intuitive touch. This occurs when you pick up or place your hands on an object and know things about it through only your touch. While any part of the hand can be used for this, humans generally receive this information through their palms. It differs from clairsentience in that you must physically touch some-thing in order to obtain information, whereas clairsentience relies on your inner feeling. Energy workers often have highly engaged clairtangency as they use their hands for healing. For example, as a Reiki practitioner places their hands on the body, they pick up information about the part of the body or chakra they're on. This is also how they can decipher which chakras are blocked or flowing and then act accordingly.

Chapter 8

Strengthening Your Third Eye

To understand the connection between your third eye and your intuition, we must first look more closely at the chakra system. The word *chakra* is a Sanskrit word that translates to "wheel" or "disk." These ever-moving energy wheels regulate different areas of the body as they correlate to each chakra. Some believe they regulate the way your spirit moves throughout your human body. During your everyday life, your chakras are constantly spinning. However, the strength with which they spin can be heightened or slowed based upon what's going on in your life. Chakras can become weak or even blocked if there are certain parts of your life you happen to be neglecting.

A BRIEF HISTORY OF
THE CHAKRA SYSTEM

The concept of chakras dates back to ancient times and is included in many cultural traditions. The first mention of chakras can be found in the Vedas, religious scriptures that are the basis of Hinduism. It's believed they originated in India in 1550 B.C. These holy texts refer to the seven chakras as "cakras."

A couple thousand years later, between 100 B.C. and A.D. 1100, the Yoga Upanishads were written. These texts referred to the chakra system as psychic centers of consciousness. A few thousand years ago, the practice of traditional Chinese medicine began, which incorporates the chakra system into its system of energy channels and meridians.

In the West, a 1919 book titled *The Serpent Power* by Arthur Avalon (a pseudonym for Sir John Woodroffe) was published. It translated two ancient Indian texts, Sat-Cakra-Nirupana and Padaka-Pancaka, into English. These texts spoke of the chakra centers in relation to Shaktic and Tantric thought. Chakras were later popularized in Western cultures through the spread of Kundalini yoga and Tantric practices.

HOW CHAKRAS WORK

There are seven main chakras in your body. These energy vortexes connect and flow into each other, acting as a channel for their energy to flow throughout the body. The vortexes themselves tend to be approximately two to four inches in size.

To visualize them, think of a spinning, three-dimensional wheel at the chakra point. You could also think of them as flowing whirlpools of light. Chakras are often depicted as lotus flowers, and each chakra has a different number of petals. Using this visualization, you could think of your spine as the "stem" and the chakras as flowers blooming from it.

These chakras overlay the human body, fusing the spiritual dimension with the physical. It's their job to keep the human body functioning in the best way possible by taking in new energy, incorporating it into our life being, and releasing old energy. It's a constant process—the "wheels" are always turning—that occurs whether you realize it's happening or not. Chakras regulate the life force energy inside us, which is also referred to as prana energy or chi.

When we talk about the chakras, we're generally speaking about the seven main chakras, though it's believed there are as many as 114 chakra centers in the body. Others believe there could be thousands and that the Earth itself has chakras all over the planet! Each chakra "rules" a specific area of your mind, body, and spirit and should be maintained regularly. Consider a cluttered home: When you spend time cleaning it up—putting everything back in its rightful place, throwing things away, removing dirt and dust—you're rewarded with an open flow of physical space afterward. (The same logic behind clearing a space that we discussed in Chapter 4 applies to this metaphor.) It's pretty much the same for the chakra system: When you clean out old and stagnant energy, you allow fresh, new energy to come in.

Chakras regulate the life force energy inside us, which is also referred to as prana energy or chi.

Following are the seven main chakras:

- **The Root Chakra:** Known as *Muladhara* in Sanskrit, the root chakra sits at the bottom of your spine or perineum. It is a red color. The root chakra is tied to your courage and self-preservation. It represents the foundation of your life, controlling basic needs like security, the home you live in, the food you eat, how much money you have, and how safe you feel. It's said to regulate your legs, feet, base of the spine, and hip areas.

- **The Sacral Chakra:** Known as *Swadhisthana* in Sanskrit, the sacral chakra can be found just below your navel. It is orange. The sacral chakra is tied to your creativity. It controls your sexual well-being, sense of pleasure, and abundance in your life. It controls your reproductive organs, intestines, bladder, and lower lymphatic system.

- **The Solar Plexus Chakra:** Known as *Manipura* in Sanskrit, the solar plexus chakra can be found above your stomach, near the upper abdomen. It is yellow. The solar plexus chakra is tied to your power. This chakra directly correlates to your self-esteem, self-acceptance, and self-confidence. It oversees the stomach, pancreas, liver, spleen, gallbladder, and adrenal glands.

- **The Heart Chakra:** Known as *Anahata* in Sanskrit, the heart chakra is right where you'd expect—your chest. It is green. The heart chakra represents love. It represents all matters of the heart, such as compassion, forgiveness, acceptance, and unconditional love. This chakra connects the lower three chakras, having to do with our earthly lives, with the top three chakras, having to do with our spiritual lives. It regulates your shoulders, arms, circulatory system, and everything in the chest (lungs, ribs, diaphragm, breasts, heart).

- **The Throat Chakra:** Known as *Vishuddha* in Sanskrit, the throat chakra is located at—you guessed it—your throat. It is blue. The throat chakra represents expression. It regulates communication, the truth, and how you assert yourself. It manages your neck, thyroid, and everything in your mouth (teeth, gums, tongue).

- **The Third Eye Chakra:** Known as *Ajna* in Sanskrit, the third eye chakra is located above your eyebrows in the middle of your forehead. It is indigo. The third eye chakra, as we've touched on in earlier chapters, is all about your intuition, vision, and wisdom. It controls your eyes, ears, nose, lower brain area, and nervous system.

- **The Crown Chakra:** Known as *Sahaswara* in Sanskrit, the crown chakra is located at the top of your head. It is violet. The crown chakra is tied to wisdom. This chakra represents your connection to your higher self and the Divine. It's connected to your skeletal and muscular systems, skin, and upper brain area.

These main chakras regulate specific areas in your life, both physically and spiritually. They can contribute to your overall well-being (or lack thereof, if they're overactive or unbalanced) and even represent the path you're on in life and how much you've awakened spiritually so far. If you've found a correlation between specific chakras and certain feelings or events happening in your life, it may be a good idea to spend some time on that particular chakra and give it some TLC. We'll dive deeper into this concept further in this chapter.

THE IMPORTANCE OF THE THIRD EYE CHAKRA FOR SPIRITUAL JOURNEYS

One of the major ways we receive spiritual information like the Akashic Records is through the chakra system, particularly the third eye chakra. This chakra, the sixth, is also known as the "inner eye" or the "brow" chakra. It's referred to as *Ajna* in Sanskrit, which loosely translates to "monitoring center." It's located right above our eyes and is often depicted in art or drawings about an inch or two above the brow line. Its close proximity to the brain, pituitary gland, and pineal gland is why it's considered to be the chakra most connected with the mind, and yet also with sight.

The third eye chakra is the center of your intuition, truth, vision, wisdom, and knowledge—all the powerful tools you'll use to receive answers during your Akashic Records session. The color associated with the third eye chakra is indigo, a bright bluish-purple color. Of all the chakras in the human energy body system, the third eye chakra will assist you the most on your spiritual journey. As the sixth chakra, it is a gateway to higher consciousness, one stop before the crown (seventh) chakra, the one through which you can obtain spiritual fulfillment and divine knowledge.

The third eye chakra is the center of your intuition, truth, vision, wisdom, and knowledge—all the powerful tools you'll use to receive answers during your Akashic Records session.

When the third eye chakra is open, one experiences deep intuition, clairvoyance, imagination, and a general sense of peace and knowing. An underactive or blocked third eye chakra can cause you to experience cloudy judgment, memory loss, and a lack of focus. On the other hand, an overactive third eye chakra can cause your mind to be restless and always in overdrive, making it difficult to concentrate. This can lead to anxiety, migraines, and even insomnia. For optimal performance during an Akashic Records session, you'll want to have this chakra cleansed, strengthened, and ready to go.

The Pineal Gland and Its Connection to the Third Eye

To fully understand the third eye chakra, we must also look at the pineal gland. It's an endocrine organ located deep in the center of the brain's cerebral cortex, tucked between the two hemispheres of the brain right where they connect. The name of the pea-sized gland is derived from the fact that it's shaped like a pinecone. Today, scientists believe its main function is to produce melatonin, which regulates sleep patterns and circadian rhythms. It uses light input to produce a schedule for releasing melatonin, distributing more at night and blocking its release during the day. This cycle of production ramps up as it gets darker at night and slowly decreases once you've fallen asleep. However, many people believe this is just the tip of the iceberg when it comes to what the pineal gland's functions are.

The pineal gland is full of lore and mystery, due largely in part to the fact that its function was discovered much later than the rest of the glands in the body. In the 1649 book *The Passions of the Soul,* French philosopher René Descartes describes it as the location of the soul. In the late nineteenth century, writer Georges Bataille wrote of the "pineal-eye." Around that same time, Helena Petrovna Blavatsky was the first to connect the pineal gland with the concept of the third eye chakra. Today, scientists are still studying this special endocrine gland, trying to figure out what mysteries could be inside. One thought, as Professor Rick Strassman of the University of New Mexico School of Medicine believes, is that it could be capable of producing hallucinations by releasing DMT (N,N-Dimethyltryptamine).

In spirituality, the pineal gland is hugely important for many reasons:

- It represents the third eye chakra, your intuition, and your inner wisdom. It is seen as a portal of sorts that will take you to a higher dimension necessary for spiritual connection and growth.

- It's the gateway to achieving clairvoyance or the tool you channel when using your clairvoyance.

- It is believed to be what perceives the visions we see *without* using our eyes. Although we haven't yet proven where psychic seeing occurs, many signs point to the pineal gland.

- It is also believed to be the first "eyes" human beings ever had, long before we developed actual eyeballs in our head.

It's clearly a very important chakra.

WAYS TO STRENGTHEN YOUR THIRD EYE CHAKRA

Your chakras constantly spin, but if they become blocked or underutilized, they may spin slowly and/or out of sync with the rest of your chakras. If your third eye chakra is out of balance or if there's something you haven't yet connected with, you probably won't be able to physically "see" during your Akashic reading session. Don't feel dismayed if this happens—many, if not most, people see nothing during their sessions. That said, if psychic sight is something you truly desire, you can certainly take action to strengthen this chakra.

The first step to strengthening and balancing your third eye is to determine why it might be out of sync. If you find that you often experience fear of the unknown and lack intuition, you might have an underactive third eye chakra. On the other hand, if you're judgmental, analytical, or overwhelmed, you may have an overactive third eye chakra. You will have a much easier time accessing and seeing the Records if you address these issues beforehand.

If your third eye chakra is out of balance or if there's something you haven't yet connected with, you probably won't be able to physically "see" during your Akashic reading session.

To get your third eye (or any) chakra back in action, there are a variety of exercises to try:

- **Use visualizations until it gets stronger.** For example, you could envision the chakra in question being cleansed or focus on the color associated with that chakra.

- **Wear the colors associated with the chakra.** There are many ways to do this, such as clothing, jewelry, or a number of other items to wear. For your third eye, wear blue or purple.

- **Try sound or singing.** You can cleanse your chakras via sound as each chakra has a different frequency. Singing bowls and sound healing help to do this but singing tones that correspond to each of the chakras is also very cleansing. Look online for more information on this topic.

- **Repeat some mantra affirmations.** Repeating phrases out loud is an excellent way to forge a stronger connection with your chakra. For the third eye chakra, saying things like "I trust my intuition" or "I see" out loud can help strengthen your bond with it. (See the following sidebar for additional mantras that can help strengthen your third eye.)

- **Meditate.** Spending time thinking about, meditating on, or intending to strengthen your connection to the third eye can also help increase your intuition.

- **Practice crystal healing.** This can be done by holding certain stones in your hand or by lying down and placing them on the chakra.

For example, for your third eye, place a blue, purple, or indigo crystal on your forehead. You can choose any stones you like that fall within that color palate, but if you're looking for suggestions, you might try amethyst, lapis lazuli, sodalite, blue kyanite, purple fluorite, azurite, purple charoite, blue aventurine, and dumortierite. Stones that work excellently with the third eye chakra but are not in the same color family include sugilite, moonstone, iolite, quartz, labradorite, moldavite, and lithium quartz.

- **Eat natural foods of that chakra's color.** For the third eye chakra, you'll want to focus on items that are blue and purple. Here's a list to get you started: plums, eggplants, purple cabbage, blueberries, blackberries, purple grapes, eggplant, figs, purple carrots, black currants, blue corn, raisins, and purple cauliflower.

- **Experiment with herbs and essential oils.** To strengthen your third eye, try using lavender, rosemary, juniper, oregano, clary sage, and mugwort. These can be diffused as essential oils, placed around the home as dried herbs, or, in some cases, eaten with food.

Mantras to Strengthen Your Third Eye

Remember, mantras are simple sounds, words, or phrases you can repeat over and over to aid in concentration and/or meditation. The following are helpful in meditations focused on your third eye.

- "I see."

- "I am wise."

- "I am intuitive."

- "I trust my intuition."

- "Intuition flows freely through me."

- "I am connected to my inner vision."

- "I see everything I am meant to."

- "My intuition guides me."

- "My third eye is strong."

- "My vision is growing."

Working on your chakras takes work and isn't something you can improve overnight. However, repeated practice helps make the changes you desire, and the long-term effects are cumulative—so you don't need to do these practices every day to reap the benefits.

Chapter 9
Understanding the Astral Plane and Spirit Guides

Now that you've learned how to get into the right mindset, connect with your third eye chakra, and choose which method makes the most sense for you, it's time to go deeper into the preparations to access the Records. In this chapter, we'll discuss how exactly to access the astral plane and your spirit guides: your gateways to the Akashic Records.

UNDERSTANDING
THE ASTRAL PLANE

Before you can begin to comprehend the location of the Akashic Records, you should first understand the astral plane itself. The astral plane, like the Akashic Records, is difficult to explain in words. It's another dimension that your soul can travel to via spiritual practices such as astral projection. It's a place where you can meet your departed loved ones to speak with them again, perhaps to heal intergenerational traumas, or simply give them a hug. You can also meet your spirit guides and communicate with them in this dimension.

In spirituality, the astral plane is known as the fourth dimension and connects to the fourth chakra, aka the heart chakra. It has also been referred to as the "World of Celestial Spheres," meaning that the soul passes through this astral dimension before being born into the world and again after death. In ancient Greece, Aristotle believed that the Celestial Spheres were made entirely of aether, a fifth element they believed existed beyond the Earth's atmosphere.

There are many theories about the astral dimension. Some people believe it's actually where our souls go to live after we leave Earth. Some think that heaven and hell are nothing more than the astral realm itself, while others believe these are two very distinct locations. It's also believed that the highest of vibrational beings live here, such as archangels and spirits.

The astral plane has multiple levels within it, all separated by different vibrational frequencies. The higher your energetic vibration, the higher into the realm you'll be able to go. For humans, that means practicing raising your energetic vibrations will allow you to access higher and higher realms. You can practice via meditation, energy healing, prayer, and by doing energetic practices such as Reiki.

The astral plane has multiple levels within it, all separated by different vibrational frequencies. The higher your energetic vibration, the higher into the realm you'll be able to go.

The ancient philosopher Plato helped to explain this plane of existence when he suggested there is more to reality than what we can see with our eyes. In "The Allegory of the Cave," Plato paints a picture of prisoners chained in a dark cave for their entire lives, unable to turn their heads to see anything. If people behind the prisoners used a candle to make shadow puppets with their hands, the prisoners would believe them to be real as their worldview (what they can see) doesn't allow them to see the candle or the puppeteers. They only see the shadows and interpret them to be real. If the puppeteers were to carry a shadow book, the prisoners would look at it and believe it to be a real book.

Plato points out that, while the prisoners are wrong in their interpretation, their experience with the shadows of books is an exercise in our perception of the physical world. Those trapped in the cave have a different perception of reality, meaning that just because they can't see something or don't know it exists, doesn't mean it doesn't exist outside the cave. This in turn relates to the astral realm: Just because you can't see it with your eyes doesn't mean it doesn't exist. The everyday non-spiritual person has no reason to believe this plane exists or to even think about it, but just because they don't know about or believe in it doesn't mean it doesn't exist.

WHAT ARE SPIRIT GUIDES?

Surely you've heard the term "guardian angel" before. They do exist, but not necessarily as they've been depicted in films or on TV. In reality, each and every human being has their own team of guides that is always there for us to call upon for help. Whether you realize it or not, you have multiple spirit guides with you at all times, watching you live your life, supporting you, and offering advice.

Common Types of Guides

Guides can take many forms. They may be:

- Ancestors

- Dearly departed family members

- Spirit animals

- Elementals

- Angels or archangels

- Gods or goddesses

- Other ascended masters

- Guides to which you have no relation

Some of your guides may have names; some may not. No matter who your group of guides includes, know that they are here to help you throughout your life on Earth.

HOW TO CONNECT WITH YOUR GUIDES

If you would like to meet your guides, there are many ways to do so. Note that you do not need to meet your guides in order to access the Akashic Records, but once you do make contact, they may help you along the way. Before you reach out to them, create a comfortable and relaxing space (as discussed in Chapter 4) so you don't have any distractions.

To connect with your guides, clear your mind and ask them questions. You may find success by repeating the same question over and over again or simply saying "I'm ready to meet my spirit guides" out loud. You may also decide to write down a list of questions for your guides to have on hand during your conversation. Once you've made contact, start by asking your guide what their name is or what information they would like you to know. If you like, you can ask them about their lives on Earth or where they come from. You can ask them anything that comes to mind—just make sure you ask your questions slowly and not all at once as you need to listen to and receive each answer fully.

Asking for Additional Help

If you'd like to speak with another guide in addition to the first one you meet, you can ask if there's a second guide that can better assist you with your questions.

If at first you don't make contact, try, try again. You might find that your first attempt to meet them will give you some information but not all that you'd hoped for, or you'll hear the name of one of your guides but not see what they look like, or you could even see that you have a team of multiple guides but only get to meet one.

Conduct repeated meditations and sessions because you'll get more and more information each time. You'll also find it's helpful to write down the information you get as soon as you can after your session concludes so you don't forget it. Keep a journal of your findings so you can refer back to them easily.

What to Do If You Can't Reach Your Guides

If these ideas aren't working for you despite your best efforts, you might try asking your spirit guides to connect with you in your sleep. They might also show up without you asking. Guides can often visit during your dreams and this is a very easy way to make the connection— as long as you wake up with a memory of it. It's a good idea to write down what you experienced in your dreams so you can recall them later.

If making a connection and speaking to your guides is a little too advanced at this point, you can also ask them for a sign that will show you your answer.

If making a connection and speaking to your guides is a little too advanced at this point, you can also ask them for a sign that will show you your answer. This is fun because you'll spend the next few days keeping an eye out for signals that illuminate the right path.

You might hear a song on the radio with lyrics that specifically pertain to your question, you might see an animal that relates to what you discussed, or you could see a sign that relates to a loved one who passed and is now looking over you from above. Just make sure you're open, ready, and willing to notice the signs as they come through.

Part Four

Accessing the Akashic Records

Now that you're armed with an extensive amount of knowledge about the Records and have a solid understanding of what's needed to prepare for a session, you're ready to have your first reading. Everyone has their own preferences, and an Akashic Records reading is no different. In this section, we'll highlight the variety of ways you can have a reading and what you can expect in each of them.

Chapter 10
Learning Ways to Access the Akashic Records

Finding basic ways to relax will help you move to the *next* level of relaxation, which you need in order to access the Records. Your goal is to ascend into a trancelike state. As you may have already gathered, there are many different routes to reaching your spiritual goals; reading the Akashic Records is no different. Some people prefer to take a more passive role, while others are ready to throw themselves across the metaphorical fire to get the answers they seek.

Meditation is the most popular way to go about communicating with the Records, though you might also try hypnosis. You can also consider working with a professional in the field to guide you to the Records or asking them to communicate with the guides on your behalf. Ultimately, the method you choose should make you feel relaxed and comfortable. There's no race to get there and no prize awarded for using the most extreme method. In fact, you should take your time and be gentle with yourself—especially if this is your first time.

MEDITATION

The simplest way to get to the Akashic Records is through meditation. For the inexperienced, meditation can sound intimidating, but it can truly be as easy or complex as you make it. You don't need fancy meditation mats, a renowned teacher, or to be surrounded by thousands of your fellow monks in a monastery to make it work. All you need is a place where you can sit or lie comfortably and clear your mind.

How do you get there? That, of course, is up to you. You can take any of the ideas suggested in this chapter to help you on your way. However, meditating to access the Akashic Records will be different than a standard meditation session. Instead of clearing your mind and attempting to keep it clear throughout the session, you'll be setting an intention and meditating on a specific question. This way it's completely clear to your guides and those who guard the Akashic Records exactly what answers you're seeking. You'll repeat your question over and over again until you find an answer. It's up to you if you prefer to speak the question out loud or repeat it on a loop in your head. Either way, you'll repeat it until you receive the sought-after information.

Ways to Get Comfortable for Meditation

So much of meditation is being comfortable and relaxed. You'll need to experiment with various décor and options to see what works best for you. Here are some ideas:

- Light a candle

- Wear comfy clothing

- Listen to soft music you enjoy

- Meditate in complete silence

- Try an aromatherapy diffuser or incense

- Drink calming tea beforehand

- Develop a soothing mantra to repeat

- Find a comfortable seat or pillow

- Make sure you aren't too hot or too cold

- Experiment with meditating at different times of day to see which works best for you

If all else fails, find an app to help jump-start your meditation journey.

LISTENING TO AN AUDIO RECORDING

Anyone who's tried meditation knows it can be a lot easier to reach a meditative state while being guided, whether by a teacher in a class or by listening to an audio recording at home. This is because we have the tendency to overthink things and many of us can't quiet our own thoughts for long enough to really relax. Listening to an audio recording is a very helpful way to meditate in order to reach the Akashic Records.

Most audio recordings will begin with a slow and simple breathing technique to help relax your body, which in turn signals the brain that it's an appropriate time to slow racing thoughts. After the breathing exercises, the speaker will then start prompting you to visualize a series of things—for example, a beautiful beach scene or a place that's special or relaxing to you. Once you're imagining yourself calm in this place, the speaker will take you through more visualizations that will lead you to the Akashic Records.

Not all recordings are the same, so it's always smart to do a little research before you choose one. Have you already decided on your intention for seeking the Akashic Records? Some recordings will pause to give you time to consider your intention while others will assume you've already done that work. There are many free recordings available online and on *YouTube*, which can be great, but to make sure you get one that's a good fit for you, consider:

- The length of the recording
- How many views it has
- What's said in the comments
- What the ratings are, if available

Listening to an audio recording is a very helpful way to meditate in order to reach the Akashic Records.

It's always a good idea to quickly Google the name of the person who created the recording to learn more about them and to make sure you feel aligned with their energy.

HYPNOSIS

Somewhere between watching people clucking around like chickens onstage and Catherine Keener maliciously swirling her tea in Get Out, hypnosis has picked up a bad reputation. Pop culture has made it seem sinister at times and like a joke at others. "You are getting sleeeepyyy" is not something I've ever heard a hypnotist say, yet we all associate those words with the practice. Thank goodness pocket watches have gone out of style.

The widespread fear of being hypnotized might come from an innate fear of losing control (where my fellow control freaks at?), which causes many of us to avoid hypnosis completely. Years ago, I met Grace Smith, a hypnosis expert, teacher, and all-around enthusiast, who's on a mission to make it mainstream. She explained it's not possible for another person to control your mind without your consent, whether we're talking about your subconscious or waking mind. Upon learning this, I got over my concerns and took a deep dive into the world of hypnosis. She worked with me to alleviate my anxiety, help combat stress, and create new patterns in my life that didn't involve spinning out over the everyday issues that came my way. You'c be surprised at the ways in which hypnosis can resolve destructive patte ns that have been wreaking havoc on your life.

Hypnosis can be used or many different reasons, but at the end of the day its main goal is simply to elicit a relaxed, trancelike state. Once in this state of mind, it's much easier to access information kept in deep places, whether in your own subconscious or on the astral plane.

Hypnosis can be used for many different reasons, but at the end of the day its main goal is simply to elicit a relaxed, trancelike state.

You can find many different hypnosis recordings online that will take you into this deeply relaxed state. You can also find a professional hypnotist to work with you. To find one, an Internet search is usually the best place to start. Try looking in your own town or city first, then widen the search if you can't find anyone nearby. Always check out the person's website to learn about their philosophy and be sure to check reviews from previous customers too. *Yelp*, *Google*, and other websites that allow feedback are great ways to learn about the hypnotist and if they fit your vibe.

Regardless of whether you do this on your own or with a professional, the method remains the same: Once you get into a relaxed state, repeat your question over and over again until you get an answer.

LISTENING TO BINAURAL BEATS

Another way to induce a trance is to listen to binaural beats, which is the sound your brain perceives when it hears two different frequencies in each ear at the same time. When your brain hears them both simultaneously, it sounds like an entirely different tone rather than hearing both tones separately. It's technically an illusion as the combined tone doesn't exist; your brain has created it. Binaural beats have many other benefits, such as improving concentration and focus while lowering stress and anxiety, and recordings can be found all over *YouTube*. Greenred Productions and Brainwave Music are great free accounts to start with.

VISUALIZATIONS

Using visualizations is yet another way to attain a trancelike state. You can envision yourself doing a number of things to achieve this state of being. For example, picture your body floating ever so gently in the air for a long period of time until you feel completely weightless. You can imagine yourself flying or astral projecting through the clouds, all over the globe, or in a certain place you find deeply relaxing. You can think about how it would feel if you were drifting in space, free of gravity. Visualizing differs from meditation in that it's something you can call upon at any time, like a mantra, instead of having to clear your mind and be in a trance, like in meditation.

A popular example of a visualization to induce a trance is to think of yourself walking up stairs for a long time, until you feel like you're in a trance—this is meant to feel like you're reaching higher states of consciousness the further up you walk.

COUNTING NUMBERS OR REPEATING WORDS

You can also try counting numbers from one to one thousand or counting them in a pattern over and over again. If numbers aren't appealing to you, try repeating a mantra nonstop until you feel like you're in a trance. Examples of a mantra include saying "I am completely weightless" or simply "I am in a trance."

Using a Candle for Trances

If you have a candle, an easy practice for getting into a trance is to stare at the flame for an extended period of time until you start to feel like you're seeing things in the flame. There are other, more extreme methods that were used in ancient times, like fasting, depriving yourself of sleep, or lying upside down, but I don't recommend them as there are much easier and safer ways to get there!

WORKING WITH A PROFESSIONAL

Sometimes it's much easier to put your trust in a professional who will guide you along the way. In fact, that's how I first made contact with the Akashic Records. It's a great choice if you're curious but don't feel confident or comfortable enough to proceed on your own. At the time I found out about the Akashic Records, the resources on the subject were minimal and the courses I found were way out of my budget. When I got the chance to cover the "goop Summit" in Los Angeles for my job—yes, the Gwyneth Paltrow lifestyle brand—and found out they'd be doing Akashic Records readings, I knew I had to try it.

When the Professional Acts on Your Behalf

I worked with Amor Luz Pangilinan of Infinite Akashic who talked me through the session and put me at ease. We discussed at length what I wanted to learn from the session, which turned out to be a lot. She suggested I focus on a single question to ask. When I decided what that would be, I gave her my consent to communicate with the Akashic Records on my behalf. She got to work immediately as I shut my eyes. Amor used sage and played a sound bowl to clear my mind and the energy in the room. After what felt like just a few minutes later, the music from her sound bowl ended. She gently tapped me on the shoulder to let me know the session had finished and that she had the answers I'd asked for. We spoke for some time afterward about the information she received on my behalf.

When working with an expert, you'll be astonished at the accuracy of what they can tell you about your life and the details of your previous ones. I recommend this experience for anyone who's afraid to go it alone and has access to a professional in their area. Professionals may be hard to come by in person in certain places, but don't worry—lots of guides offer virtual sessions via video or phone calls. Their expertise will be just as helpful from a distance as it is in real life.

When the Professional Guides You

Another option when working with a professional is to have them guide you along the way but let you do the communicating. Their job in this instance is to provide a comfortable environment for the session, to get you into a meditative or trancelike state, and then guide you along the journey. They may prompt you throughout each step of the process or they may say very little. It all depends on what you'd like them to do. You might want to have someone there simply to watch over the process, whereas others might want to be guided along the way. It's really a matter of personal preference and how far you've "leveled up" spiritually.

Finding Someone to Work With

To find someone to work with, the best place to start is the Internet. Most practitioners have their own websites that will explain their background and what their practice focuses on. Make sure you read through to see if they're someone you could see yourself feeling comfortable with. It's important to feel at ease around the person you're working with, and it's a good idea to take a look at the reviews previous customers have written about them. It's also helpful to read the success stories from those who've had great experiences. Working with a professional will likely set you back a couple hundred dollars.

You may find you start out working with a professional and after a couple of sessions feel comfortable enough to try the process at home on your own. There's no wrong way to get there, so be easy on yourself.

USING CRYSTALS TO ASSIST YOU

Accessing the Akashic Records requires traveling to an entirely different dimension, the astral realm. Considering this plane of existence is somewhere that's new to you, it only makes sense to bring along your favorite crystal ally for protection or strength.

Purchasing a Stone for Readings

If you're seeking out stones for an Akashic reading, you might consider setting that intention as you walk into the store or upon logging on to a website. You can say "I request a stone that will help me access the Akashic Records" in your head or repeat it as a mantra. You can also "ask" a stone when you pick it up if it will serve your needs. Hold it in your hand and ask in your head, "Will you assist me in seeking the Akashic Records?" Take a moment to feel what the answer is—if you feel a strong yes, then it's worth purchasing. A hard no or a vague answer would suggest putting the stone back on the shelf or considering it for another use.

Suggested Crystals for Beginners

- **Clear quartz:** Known as "the master healer," clear quartz is known for its versatility and availability—by some estimates, it's the most bountiful crystal on Earth. If you're looking for a crystal remedy that's essentially a one-stop shop, this stone is said to balance the physical, mental, emotional, and spiritual states of being. It can direct and amplify energy using only your intention. It's also known to draw negative energy away from the body and into the stone, transmuting the energy back into the world. Because of its cleansing properties, clear quartz can be used on any chakra. It's also a stone that can be used to clear the energy of other stones, and it never needs to be charged or cleared itself.

- **Selenite:** This stone is one of the highest vibrational stones in existence. Because of this, it's able to remove negative energy from a human being's energy body. (Maybe you've seen selenite wands used to clear a person's energy—Kylie Jenner posted a *YouTube* tutorial, after all—where someone slowly moves a long piece of selenite along someone's body to "scrape off" unwanted energy.) Selenite is also a lovely stone that aids in sleep by resolving the negative vibrations inside you while you sleep. It is also a protective stone, one that's often used in doorways or corners of rooms and houses to keep an entire space clear of negative energy. One thing to note about selenite is that it's extremely fragile and cannot get wet, so make sure you take extra caution with this extra-special stone. It's most often used with the crown chakra but can be used anywhere.

- **Amethyst:** One of the most powerful stones, amethyst is said to protect against psychic and energetic attacks by transmuting energy into love and protecting the wearer from harm. This specific stone is great for beginners as it's known to activate your spiritual awareness, open up your intuition, and enhance your psychic powers. Amethyst is often called a "natural tranquilizer," meaning that among its healing properties is the ability to help you de-stress. It's said to cleanse the body's energy field, which is ideal if you're trying to raise your vibration. This bright purple stone correlates specifically with the third eye and crown chakras and can be placed on your forehead or on the top of your head during a meditation or Akashic Records session. In everyday life, you can hold this stone in your hands for a gentle, cleansing meditation. Many choose to keep this stone in their pockets or wear it as jewelry to help them stay calm throughout the day.

- **Lapis lazuli and sodalite:** These two similar stones are most often used with the third eye and throat chakras. They both possess healing properties that include helping to strengthen your intuition, truth, and third eye connection. Sodalite and lapis lazuli also help with emotionally balancing yourself and providing clarity to any issues in or confusing parts of your life. Their bright blue colors make them some of the prettiest stones in the world. In fact, historians estimate humans have been working with these stones for more than 6,500 years, including in ancient Egypt.

- **Malachite:** A stone that rarely looks the same twice because of its unique patterning, malachite is known as a stone of transformation. It's said that malachite can heal deep emotional wounds of the heart and jump-start your passion. It's a great stone to protect and strengthen your energetic field. It's said it can also protect you from negative entities. Ancient Egyptians and Romans loved to wear this stone as an adornment. Malachite is most often used on the heart and throat chakras, though it's able to work with all seven of the main chakras. It's also lovely to look at because of the waves, lines, and circle patterns it makes as it grows.

- **Rose quartz:** Known as the stone of universal love, this stone assists with self-love, romantic love, friendships, and relationships. It is therefore a go-to crystal for all matters of the heart. Working with this stone or having it in your home helps to promote your own receptibility to love of any kind. It helps remove negative energy and replaces it with vibrations of love. If you're going through a particularly sad breakup or trauma, there's no better stone to have by your side. Rose quartz can help to release built-up thoughts and feelings from former loves, freeing up space in your heart for new love to enter. Rose quartz is most often used with the heart chakra.

- **Citrine:** This variety of quartz is known as the "success stone" or the "merchant's stone" because of its lore of being able to build wealth and bring prosperity. This translucent yellow stone is said to be emotionally balancing, motivating, and encouraging of self-expression. Since it connects to your power center, it's able to help raise a person's self-confidence and self-esteem. Like clear quartz, it can be used on many of the chakras and is said to energize all aspects of your life. Specifically, citrine is most often used on the sacral, solar plexus, and crown chakras.

- **Carnelian:** This stabilizing, grounding stone is said to help with creativity, emotional warmth, and the appreciation of nature. It can help to increase your self-esteem and promote a feeling of peace in your life. It's used most often with the sacral chakra, which is your creative center. Spending time with carnelian can help bust you out of writer's block or a creative rut. A variety of chalcedony, carnelian stones have wavy lines of color throughout.

- **Smoky quartz:** A reliable healing stone, smoky quartz—sometimes spelled smokey—is known to remove negative energy from the body. It's a great stone to keep you grounded and it prevents you from feeling overwhelmed in life. Smoky quartz is a brownish-gray color and is generally used with the root and solar plexus chakras.

- **Red jasper:** This stone is said to help ground negative energies into the Earth and calm emotions. It's known to be a protective stone that brings the wearer peace of mind. Red jasper can also bring relaxation and contentment, making it a great stone to carry on your person daily. It's said to absorb negative energy and bring nurturing healing to the body. Red jasper is mostly used with the root chakra, as it correlates with the root energy of the Earth. It can be placed anywhere from the hips down.

- **Black tourmaline:** This stone is all about bringing strength, balance, and positive transformation. A powerful stone of protection, it transmutes negative energy and blocks psychic attacks. It can help neutralize your negative thoughts, which is especially helpful when trying to fall asleep. One tip about this crystal is that, while it draws negative energy away from you, it tends to keep it inside, so it must be cleared every so often. It also doesn't do very well in water. Black tourmaline is associated with the root chakra.

Using Crystals and Charkas Together

When using crystals in an Akashic Records session, it's a smart idea to use stones that correlate to the different chakras and place them on the appropriate area of your body. To do this, think about the chakras and how they relate to your life. For example:

- If you're having trouble speaking your truth, that's a good sign that your throat chakra could be blocked and you might choose a blue stone for your throat area.

- If you've found that you're lacking personal power or motivation lately, it might be a good idea to place a yellow stone on your upper stomach for your solar plexus chakra.

When thinking about the needs of an Akashic session, you will likely include some stones for the crown chakra, since it represents the connection to the Divine, your throat chakra, so you'll be able to speak without fear, and the root chakra, as it will help you stay centered and grounded throughout the session. However, you could also include stones for every chakra, no chakras, or somewhere in between.

Crystal Grids

Crystal grids are another wonderful way to direct the flow of energy. A crystal grid is a row or arrangement of crystals that is pointing in a certain direction to maximize vibrational flow. You can make a grid that's as simple or as complicated as you like (look online for inspiration), but for accessing the Akashic Records, you'll be making a grid around either your body or the room in which you're holding your session. To make a crystal grid, you must have at least one pointed stone to use as a wand. From there, you'll arrange a bunch of crystals in some type of pattern or geometric shape. For a simple arrangement, try placing a few stones in the corners of a square, pointing inward. Or you may want to place stones around the perimeter of where you'll be lying or sitting for the session. Once they're in place, take the crystal "wand" and connect all the stones to each other energetically by moving the wand from stone to stone. As you do so, focus on your intention for your Akashic Records session. You'll be surprised at how much of an energetic charge these grids can hold!

Chapter 11
Knowing What to Expect in an Akashic Records Session

The experience of an Akashic Records session varies from person to person. We've already discussed personalizing your space, adding any spiritual accompaniments (such as candles or crystals) that resonate with you, and the many ways to clear your mind so you can enter a trancelike state. Regardless of the route you take to get there, all sessions tend to have a similar process to them. This chapter will outline that process so you know what awaits you.

THE STRUCTURE
OF THE SESSION

First, you'll want to make sure you're in a relaxed state of mind and as comfortable as possible. Second, know that everyone's experience is different. The important part is to take it slow and not rush anything. Take in as much as you can during your session. Consider the five senses: What do you see, feel, hear, taste, and smell? What emotions are you feeling? Try to keep a mental note of your observations or write them down for your next session. You may find that your visualization looks different with each visit or that it's the same every time. Again, there's no wrong way to experience the Records. Here's a general overview of what to expect.

Getting Ready

We've outlined all the different methods to connect to the Records in Chapter 10, so be sure to choose and practice how you'll make the connection ahead of time. The most common way of doing so is through guided meditation, but you may choose to use hypnosis or enter a trancelike state instead. You may also decide to seek out a spiritual professional who offers Akashic Records readings. In this case, the professional may guide you through the process or simply access your records for you. It's a good idea to discuss the visualizations they will use beforehand in case there's room to customize them or you want to share an opinion.

Going on the Journey

Once you're lying or sitting down, you'll be led through a series of guided words that will take you on your journey. Every practitioner and audio recording is different and will use different visualizations and methods. Some of them will ask you to imagine a comforting place that is special to you, while others will take you on a ride through the clouds and into the atmosphere.

Finding Your Akashic Records

At a certain point, these words will paint a picture of the Akashic Records. Some will go into great detail to help you visualize a great hall or library. They'll guide you through the doors, into the hallways lined with books, and to your personal book of information.

Asking Your Question(s)

From there, you'll be prompted to ask your question(s) and receive your answer(s). Once that portion is finished, the meditation will slowly and gently guide you back to Earth.

WHO YOU MAY MEET ALONG THE WAY

As discussed in Chapter 9, the astral plane is another dimension (the fourth, actually) where spirits, angels, and other highly vibrational beings live. You can travel to it through meditation, astral projecting, or a number of other spiritual practices outlined in this book. When you visit the great hall of the Akashic Records, keep in mind that every great library has a security team.

Yes, the Akashic Records are guarded by spirits who have been put there to preserve its sacred nature. When you communicate with the Records, you'll often be communicating through these guards. This communication can take many forms. When you first reach them, these spiritual guards will likely ask you for your full name in order to grant you clearance into the hall of records. You might vividly see the guards as you speak to them, or you might see nothing and only hear their voices. It's possible you won't see or hear anything from these guards at all but will instead be left with a deep knowing (aka claircognizance) of the answers you sought.

You may be greeted at the Records by your personal spirit guides and/or team of light. They may choose to meet you there of their own accord, or you may call them in to help you. As discussed in Chapter 9, your team of guides is always with you and always ready to assist— and what better occasion for you to call on their expertise? You can customize your experience with your guides based on your needs and preferences. You can ask them—or one of them specifically—to accompany you on your journey to the Akashic Records, or they can meet you there. You can also tell them your question in advance so they're able to help communicate with the Records. If you're feeling nervous at all, it's a great idea to ask for the protection of your guides during the whole experience. However much or little you want to call on your guides is up to you.

You may be greeted at
the Records by your
personal spirit guides
and/or team of light.

WHAT YOU MIGHT SEE

As you embark on this highly personal journey, you might see various images—or nothing at all. There's no wrong way to "see" (or not see) what you're experiencing. Everyone will imagine what the Akashic Records look like in their own way, and everything that is seen is right.

Don't Worry If You Don't See Anything

Many, if not most, people don't see anything during their Akashic reading. This could be for any number of reasons:

- Because the Records technically exist in another dimension, they are very difficult for humans to see. This doesn't mean you *can't* see them, but it is less likely.

- You don't have enough experience yet. If you haven't dabbled in many spiritual practices, it's possible you aren't as "open" to seeing as you want to be. To combat this, adopting a regular spiritual practice such as meditation can help you be more open to receiving.

- Your third eye chakra is either weak or blocked. As you know from Chapter 8, the third eye chakra is your connection to inner vision. This inner vision, for some, can actually include visuals and "seeing." The clarity of "vision" of the third eye is different for each person and depends on how spiritually in tune they are. Some of us see bright, realistic visions with all sorts of colors and patterns, some of us see basic outlines and light-forms in only one color, and some see waves of nondescript energy and patterns. The lucky ones are born with a pristine inner vision and can see it all—though they may feel as if they can't turn it off (but they can, through training). Follow the ideas for strengthening your third eye chakra in Chapter 8 to improve your clarity.

Your Visual Experience

Let's talk through what you may see during an Akashic Records session if you *do* see something. Most people use some kind of guided meditation to reach the Records. While this is a great choice, it's also likely that what you're seeing is being influenced by the visualizations being described in the recording. Listening to the description and visual cues being given to you can help paint a picture with words, and that's fine!

If you choose to use another method and don't have someone describing what you're seeing, you may find that you see something entirely of your own creation. Most meditations and guides will take you to the entrance of a building first. This is where you may see the guards of the Akashic Records. It's possible you'll have an exchange with them, but it's also possible you won't see them at all. Or maybe you've worked out a deal with your spirit guides to have them talk to the guards on your behalf. Whether you envision them to be intense or friendly, know that they are not there to do you harm.

From there, you'll move inside the building you've envisioned. Most people then picture a grand hall, a university-like setting, or simply a library. You may see something entirely different, and that's okay.

It's possible that, once inside, you'll see one giant, all-knowing book with all Records inside it. It's also possible you'll envision a gigantic hall of books, one for each soul, and you'll have to find the book specifically about you. Either way of looking at this is correct.

Once you make it to the book you want, you may envision yourself flipping through the pages or you might have an immediate connection to the book and not need to do anything further.

How to Ask Your Questions

We talked about questions to ask during your session back in Chapter 5. Now is a good time to review what you came up with and see if your top question still resonates. If it does, great! If not, feel free to tweak or revise it however you want.

One note: Don't worry too much about the specific words you're using or the exact phrasing of what to say. No matter what words you end up thinking or saying out loud in your session, know that your intention has just as much power as your actual words do. As long as your intentions are pure, you're putting out a positive vibration that goes along with it. Even if your words come out clunky, the point will still get across. Some people obsess over the nuances of the words they choose in a session and that's not necessary. Let your intentions guide the way and trust that you'll receive the answers you seek.

HOW ANSWERS MIGHT COME TO YOU

As mentioned earlier in this book, the Akashic Records are not actually records or a book at all. They are a metaphysical text that exists in another plane of existence we are lucky to be able to access at all. As such, the human mind cannot comprehend the information learned from the Records in their original form. Our brains take the experience and format it to look like what it normally understands to be a place to receive information: a hall of records and a book of text.

Be Prepared for Answers to Come in Many Ways

The answers you receive may come to you in ways you may not be used to. Every human receives information in different ways based upon a number of factors, including your mental clarity, energetic state, life situation, and the development of your clairvoyant senses. Some of you will vividly see yourself in a hall of records, flipping through the pages of an ancient text and reading your answer. Others will see nothing at all. Those who don't generally "see" an answer will receive theirs in another way, whether they hear, feel, or simply know it (via clairvoyance, clairaudience, clairsentience, or claircognizance). See Chapter 7 for a refresher on receiving information via your intuitive systems.

Every human receives information in different ways based upon a number of factors, including your mental clarity, energetic state, life situation, and the development of your clairvoyant senses.

In addition to receiving answers in ways you weren't expecting, you may be given a small amount of information during your session with more coming later. Not every reading provides a heavy downpour of answers. You may get a lot of information, a little, or none at all. You may also be sent signals through objects, places, or people that provide the answers you're looking for. The signs might be new information to you or a reminder of what you heard in your reading. For example, if you learned in a reading that you lived a previous life in ancient Rome, you may discover the next day that you'll be going on a field trip to study that exact subject. Or, if you learned you were an artist in a previous life, you may be given art supplies out of nowhere from a friend or relative. All these signs are there to encourage your spiritual seeking and show that you're on the right path.

Keep a Journal

Write down everything you learn during or after a session in a journal. Information may come to you in pieces, so it's helpful to have all the information in one place, regardless of when it arrives. This way you can look back at it holistically and draw your conclusions. You may pick up on certain patterns or piece things together you wouldn't have otherwise had they not been written down. If you choose not to write anything down, you may forget important details or, worse, forget the information you received entirely.

Your Answers May Come at a Different Time

You may find yourself disappointed with the lack of information received during a reading, but go to bed that night and you may learn much more in a dream. Spirit guides in particular like to communicate with humans in their dream states. It's a particularly helpful time because, while sleeping, your body is in a calm, receptive state. Your train of thoughts has ended, leaving your mind time to explore, refresh, and comprehend everything that happened that day. This is the perfect time for you to receive messages from your spirit guides, angels, or the Akashic Records. (It's a good idea to write down what you saw as soon as you wake up the next morning so you don't forget anything.)

You may also receive downloads of information in the days following an Akashic reading. This is common among claircognizant people, who receive their spiritual insights through a sense of knowing and not necessarily through intuitive vision. You could be walking down the street and suddenly get a jolt of knowledge about a past life or a question facing you in this one.

Chapter 12
Troubleshooting If You Didn't Receive Answers

If you've tried the recommendations in this book and have yet to make a connection to the Akashic Records, have no fear. This is entirely common. There are other obstacles to consider that might be standing in your way. The answers may also appear in your everyday life in unexpected ways. In this chapter, we'll go through a troubleshooting of sorts to identify what might clear your path to the Akashic Records.

TRY A DIFFERENT
METHOD OF ACCESS

First, let's examine some of the possibilities as to why you haven't made a connection. A quick fix is to change the method you tried. For example:

- If you used solo meditation for entering a trancelike state, you might want to try a guided audio recording instead. Guided audio also helps your mind to relax and follow the instructions.

- If you tried guided audio and liked the format but not the execution, switch to a different recording until you find one that really resonates with you.

- If none of the methods you're trying alone are working, it may be worth seeking out a professional who can help.

CONSIDER YOUR
PHYSICAL STATE

Another major variable in the process is whether or not you're under the influence of a substance.

Were You Drinking Alcohol?

Alcohol is of no service to you on your spiritual path. It is a depressant, after all. Not only does it lower your energetic vibration; it also makes your mind very cloudy, which is the opposite of what you want. You want your mind to be as clear as possible when connecting to the Akashic Records. Plus, alcohol causes foggy memories or complete blackouts, which are not helpful considering you're seeking answers you'd like to remember! We already know alcohol can cause liver damage, inflammation, brain damage, and a weakening of the immune system, so it's not serving your physical body either.

Spiritually, it's believed drinking alcohol can cause holes in your aura and disrupt the energetic flow of your chakras. Some believe drinking to intoxication can cause your spirit to leave your physical body, leaving room for dark entities to enter in its place. These dark spirits then push us to act in ways we never would if we were sober. While this theory may be a stretch to some, we have all seen someone's—or our own—behaviors, speech, or actions change as a result of drinking alcohol. Is it really so far-fetched to imagine that, when imbibing alcohol, we're harming ourselves spiritually?

Were You Using Drugs?

Drugs can affect your mind adversely too. Marijuana can sometimes assist in spiritual work because of how it opens up the mind, but it can make it hard to focus, which you need to do in an Akashic reading. It can also cause your mind to feel fuzzy, spacey, or leave you thinking that everything is funny. At its worst, it can cause extreme paranoia and fear—both of which will bring your spiritual work to a stop.

When speaking of drugs, we must also talk about prescribed drugs and medicines you get over the counter. If you've found you cannot communicate spiritually, whether it be with the Akashic Records, your guides, or otherwise, you may want to take a look at the side effects of any medicines you're taking. If you find there are side effects that could be messing with your spiritual connection, like headaches, fatigue, or dizziness, talk to your doctor about the possibility of making changes to your prescriptive regimen.

TRY AGAIN TO BECOME
FULLY RELAXED

Another possibility as to why you can't connect to the Records is that your mind may not be fully relaxed. Here are some common reasons people aren't able to relax enough to access the Records.

Calm a Busy Mind

Our lives are busy, and so are our brains. If you have trouble turning that off, it may be standing in your way. A racing mind may seem productive at first, but in reality, it's a nonstop cycle of never-ending thoughts that your mind has to deal with, which never allows for peace. If you can't stop this constant parade of thoughts in your head, you're likely overwhelmed, overstimulated, or overcommitted.

A racing mind may seem productive at first, but in reality, it's a nonstop cycle of never-ending thoughts that your mind has to deal with, which never allows for peace.

If this is the first time you've realized you have racing thoughts you can't control, you may want to take a look at what could be causing this and try to make some changes:

- If you're overwhelmed, check in with your feelings. It's important to keep track of your emotions and take care of them. If you feel like your emotions are spiraling out of control, take some time to breathe, relax, and/or sit in your emotions until you reach some clarity.

- If you're overstimulated, consider monitoring or reducing your screen time.

- If you're overcommitted, you should know that it's fully okay to say no to things—people will understand that you have too much on your plate.

Focus On Your Breathing

What are the best ways to quiet your mind and relax your body? That depends on your needs and preferences. Deep breathing and controlled breathing exercises are one of the easiest—and cheapest, considering it's free—ways to calm your brain. Revisit the suggestions in Chapter 6 for information on and recommendations for breathing exercises. Here are two quick ideas:

1. Count to four or eight as you breathe in and out. You can add a hold at the end of breathing in and at the end of breathing out to make it a longer, slower process.
2. Focus on one specific area or part of the body while breathing. Common areas to focus on include the place where the air meets your nose, your lungs as they fill with air, or your stomach as it rises and falls with each breath. You'll find that, as you focus on these, your brain and body will start to relax.

If thoughts pop into your head while you're practicing breathing, simply note that thoughts have come into your mind, let them pass, and refocus on breathing. Breathing this way is excellent during times of stress, and doing it regularly is helpful to your overall well-being.

Meditate or Exercise

Meditation is an excellent choice for calming the mind. The very practice is an exercise in choosing peace over the busy thoughts running through your head. You may choose to practice at home in silence, by listening to a guided meditation, or by checking out a meditation studio to see what it's like.

If standard meditation isn't for you, you could try something that has a more physical element to it like yoga, Pilates, or simply working out. Yoga is deeply tied to spirituality and the chakra system and can be an extraordinary method of spiritual work. Exercise of any kind is a great way to expel old energy and recharge your body. If you can create a full exercise routine you can memorize, that can be a meditation of its own kind because your brain will relax and enter a receptive state while your body is doing tasks it knows well. Regular or daily practice can contribute to both your physical and mental well-being.

Exercise of any kind is
a great way to expel old
energy and recharge
your body.

BE SURE YOU SET A CLEAR INTENTION

Before an Akashic reading—or any spiritual work, really—you should set an intention for what you expect to happen next. You can do this through prayer, a mantra, writing it down in a journal, or saying the words out loud. When you put your intentions out into the universe, you're more likely to receive what you want. For an Akashic reading, your intention might be along the lines of "I intend to connect with my guides to access the Akashic Records without distraction." Or maybe you want to use a short mantra you can repeat out loud, such as "My mind is calm and I am ready to receive." If you gave this part of the process short shift, revisit Chapter 5 and create an intention and question that will bolster your efforts.

BE PATIENT

As discussed in Chapter 11, it's common to not immediately get answers during a session. While this is extremely frustrating, you must first understand that spiritual work is a long process and you simply might not be ready to receive the answers you seek. You might have all the information you need in your subconscious but it's waiting to reveal itself until you're ready. It could be revealed to you soon or perhaps much later in your life.

Your spirit guides are also always looking out for you, monitoring your spiritual growth and cheering you on from the sidelines. They know what you can or cannot handle and would never present you with information they didn't think you could take, so they might hold back information until a more beneficial time.

Your spirit guides are also always looking out for you, monitoring your spiritual growth and cheering you on from the sidelines.

The bottom line is to be patient. It's possible you won't get any answers during your session but will receive information downloads via signs in your everyday life or in a dream. Trust in the process and that all will be revealed in time.

ASK YOURSELF
IF YOU ARE AFRAID

If none of the ideas in this chapter register for you as an issue, your blocks could be fear-based. You may be fearful of what your Akashic reading will uncover, either consciously or unconsciously. If so, remember that your guides are always looking out for you and will only present you with the knowledge that will serve you best at that time.

You might worry you aren't good enough or worthy of such divine knowledge. This is entirely untrue. We are all divine beings, entitled to the highest information and the happiest of lives.

Living in fear is a surefire way to stunt your spiritual growth. Fear is the opposite of love. In spirituality, fear is seen as an illusion. Fear drags you down and causes you to downplay your personal power. It causes you to think you're unworthy or unable to live out your dreams. You can't control everything in your life—let alone the world or universe—and trying to do so is an exercise in futility. The more you can roll with the punches and accept that everything in your life—good and bad—can be worked through and learned from, the less you will live in fear.

CONCLUSION

And there you have it—everything you need to know about getting started with the Akashic Records. You've learned:

- What they are and where they exist, including that they aren't physically accessible here on Earth.

- The different ways in which you can access the Records for yourself, either through meditation, entering a trance, working with a professional, or other creative methods of getting to them.

- The ways in which you can adjust your space, like making sure it's comfortable and undisturbed, to optimize it for your readings.

- Techniques for "getting in the zone," whether you prefer breathing exercises or working with crystals.

- What types of questions you can ask in your readings and how to set intentions to help with your desired result.

- How to troubleshoot if you find yourself blocked from accessing the Records.

Now that you understand what they are, you can use the Akashic Records to assist you on your life's journey. After you've accessed the Records once, you'll find it much easier to visit them again. In times of struggle, fear, or even self-reflection, know that you can always call on them for assistance. This sacred, infinite amount of information is readily available for your use at any time. No question is too small or insignificant to call upon the Records for help. It is your divine right as a spiritual human being to access this information. May you use it during times of need to guide you on your way and in times of self-exploration to help you discover your path forward in this lifetime.

Index

Flowers, 72, 79, 83, 106, 129. *See also* Herbs
Fourth dimension, 144, 175–76

Get Out, 160
Goals
  for Akashic Records sessions, 25–26, 173–84
  determining, 25
  intentions and, 25–26, 88–89
  material gains and, 60
  spiritual goals, 155
  writing, 98
Gods/goddesses, 122, 147
Grounding techniques, 41
Guardian angels, 146–47. *See also* Spirit guides
Gut feelings, 18, 95, 115, 119. *See also* Clairvoyance; Intuitive systems

Heart chakra, 38–39, 131–32
Herbs
  chakras and, 140
  choosing, 77–79
  descriptions of, 77–79
  metaphysical properties of, 77
  positive energy of, 83
  purchasing, 40
  scent of, 72
  for smudging, 40, 76–83
Home. *See also* Space
  cleansing rituals for, 81–83
  decluttering, 76–77, 85, 129
  décor for, 70–71
  distractions in, 24, 69–70, 100
  lighting in, 71
  peace in, 70–71
  scent of, 71–72

smudging techniques, 72, 74–83
supplies for, 70–71
temperature of, 71
Hypnosis, 18, 25, 156, 160–62, 174. *See also* Trancelike states

Illusion, 23
Incarnation, 9, 15, 57–60. *See also* Past life; Reincarnation
Incense, 72, 108–9
Intentions
  creating, 88–89
  determining, 88–89
  envisioning, 88–89
  explanation of, 88
  goals and, 25–26, 88–89
  keeping track of, 98
  mantras for, 97–98, 194
  questions to ask, 88–94
  setting, 25–26, 87–98, 194
  wording of, 95–96
Intuitive systems
  chakras and, 127–28
  clairalience, 125
  clairaudience, 122–23
  claircognizance, 123–24
  clairempathy, 122
  clairgustance, 125
  clairsentience, 119–22
  clairtangency, 125–26
  clairvoyance, 115–19
  spiritual connections, 115–26
Isis Unveiled, 21

Jenner, Kylie, 167
Journal, keeping, 29, 92, 97, 98, 149, 183, 194

Discover the Power of Starseeds!

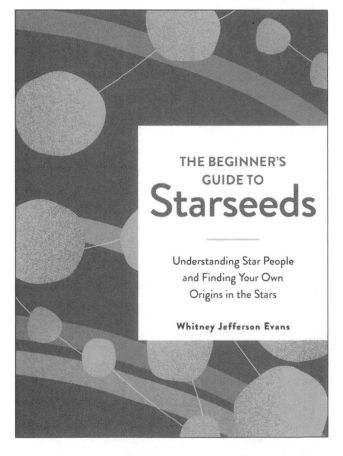

THE BEGINNER'S
GUIDE TO
Starseeds

Understanding Star People
and Finding Your Own
Origins in the Stars

Whitney Jefferson Evans

Pick Up or Download Your Copy Today!